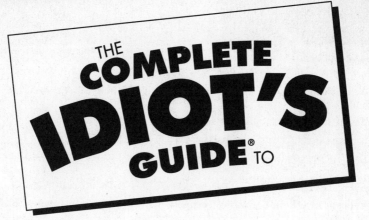

THE COMPLETE IDIOT'S GUIDE® TO

Cheese Making

by James R. Leverentz

ALPHA

A member of Penguin Group (USA) Inc.

ALPHA BOOKS

Published by the Penguin Group

Penguin Group (USA) Inc., 375 Hudson Street, New York, New York 10014, USA

Penguin Group (Canada), 90 Eglinton Avenue East, Suite 700, Toronto, Ontario M4P 2Y3, Canada (a division of Pearson Penguin Canada Inc.)

Penguin Books Ltd., 80 Strand, London WC2R 0RL, England

Penguin Ireland, 25 St. Stephen's Green, Dublin 2, Ireland (a division of Penguin Books Ltd.)

Penguin Group (Australia), 250 Camberwell Road, Camberwell, Victoria 3124, Australia (a division of Pearson Australia Group Pty. Ltd.)

Penguin Books India Pvt. Ltd., 11 Community Centre, Panchsheel Park, New Delhi—110 017, India

Penguin Group (NZ), 67 Apollo Drive, Rosedale, North Shore, Auckland 1311, New Zealand (a division of Pearson New Zealand Ltd.)

Penguin Books (South Africa) (Pty.) Ltd., 24 Sturdee Avenue, Rosebank, Johannesburg 2196, South Africa

Penguin Books Ltd., Registered Offices: 80 Strand, London WC2R 0RL, England

International Standard Book Number: 978-1-61564-009-6
Library of Congress Catalog Card Number: 2009938587

12 11 10   8 7 6 5 4 3 2

Interpretation of the printing code: The rightmost number of the first series of numbers is the year of the book's printing; the rightmost number of the second series of numbers is the number of the book's printing. For example, a printing code of 10-1 shows that the first printing occurred in 2010.

Printed in the United States of America

Note: This publication contains the opinions and ideas of its author. It is intended to provide helpful and informative material on the subject matter covered. It is sold with the understanding that the author and publisher are not engaged in rendering professional services in the book. If the reader requires personal assistance or advice, a competent professional should be consulted.

Most Alpha books are available at special quantity discounts for bulk purchases for sales promotions, premiums, fundraising, or educational use. Special books, or book excerpts, can also be created to fit specific needs.

For details, write: Special Markets, Alpha Books, 375 Hudson Street, New York, NY 10014.

Publisher: *Marie Butler-Knight*
Editorial Director: *Mike Sanders*
Senior Managing Editor: *Billy Fields*
Acquisitions Editor: *Tom Stevens*
Development Editor: *Susan Zingraf*
Production Editor: *Kayla Dugger*

Copy Editor: *Sonja Nikkila*
Cover Designer: *Bill Thomas*
Book Designer: *Trina Wurst*
Indexer: *Heather McNeill*
Layout: *Ayanna Lacey*
Proofreader: *Laura Caddell*

Contents at a Glance

Contents

Appendixes

Introduction

There are two things you must know about cheese making before anything in this book will make sense. First, cheese making, on any scale, is chemistry and biology, not cooking or baking. Second, cheese making requires artful skills born of attentive patience. The blending of science and art into the process of changing milk into cheese is as close to culinary alchemy as you can get. This book is meant to teach you both the technology and art of personal cheese making in an entertaining and appetizing way.

The first cheese I tried to make was cheddar. It took the better part of a day to prepare the cheese and a week to get it ready for waxing, followed by months of aging and anticipating the final results. In the end, the cheese was moldy, flavorless, dry, and crumbly. My mistake was starting in the middle and working in two directions at once. Knowledge of cheese making starts at the beginning and builds on the foundation of experience. It is not that making cheese is difficult. Making cheese is different.

Do not look at this book as a cookbook-style collection of cheese-making recipes. Most common cookbooks and many cheese-making volumes are written so that each recipe is independent of the others. These books also include assumptions, with a few notable exceptions, of the reader's subject knowledge and basic cooking skills. Teaching you to make your own cheese requires that no assumptions be made and that you will travel through the chapters of this book in the order they are presented. You must be able to assess each new recipe process with the background and experience you will have gained from preceding recipes.

If a comparison of cheese making and another culinary effort is needed, it would have to be with the brewing of beer. Beer is made of four primary ingredients (water, malt, hops, and yeast), yet there are over 6,000 documented styles of beer worldwide. It is the brewmaster's skill at manipulating these ingredients that makes one beer different from another. The seasoned cheesemaker also uses four primary ingredients (dairy milk, microorganisms, enzymes, and salt), yet is capable of producing over 3,000 documented cheese styles in the United States alone. In both brewing and cheese making, the secrets to success are in the process rather than the recipe.

Making cheese in your kitchen is not unlike making it in a creamery or factory. The ingredients are the same. The terminology used to describe the process is the same. Even the need for strict sanitation and environmental controls are the same. The most notable difference is your source of raw material. All of the recipes given here are formulated to be made with store-bought cow's milk. Yes, the milk at the supermarket can be used to make very good cheese. These recipes will also work equally as well or better with fresh milk from dairy animals, provided that the milk is cared for properly.

The greatest difference between your kitchen cheese and commercial creamery cheese will be the volume of milk used and therefore the amount of cheese produced by a single batch. The included recipes have been formulated based on two critical factors. First is the minimum amount of milk that can be used to produce a satisfactory cheese, and second is the maximum amount of milk that can be easily managed in the average kitchen using household-size utensils.

You will start your cheese-making adventure by making very simple, yet tasty and useful, cheeses made from store-bought dairy products. You will then progress through the entire collection of cheese styles, including soft cheese, semi-hard cheese, ripened cheese, hard cheese, and aged cheese. Each cheese-making session will combine experiences from previous recipes and introduce new techniques and/or the use of new ingredients.

Some cheeses you may want to make simply cannot be created on a small scale. Swiss cheese, with its signature large holes (called eyes), requires a wheel size of 10 to 20 pounds to provide space for the eyes to grow. Parmesan requires raw milk and takes over a year to produce. Rather than dedicate valuable space to "facsimiles" of these cheeses, I have limited the variety of cheese recipes to cover popular styles that teach the methodology of cheese making. You may not find the recipe you are looking for, but you will learn the cheese-making techniques and skills needed to produce it. You will be learning valuable skills that may lead you to new pastures (pun intended), but please note that the information given here is in no way a comprehensive representation of the cheese-making art.

Knowing how to use the finished cheese is as important as being able to make it. Recipes for dishes ranging from snacks to desserts are included for each cheese type. You will learn to recognize and exploit the special characteristics and flavors of all cheese styles.

If your interest in cheese making is purely academic and you never actually make your own cheese, by reading this book you will gain an insightful appreciation for the art of cheese making and an increased understanding of the unique textures and delicious flavors within a given cheese.

How This Book Is Organized

Cheese making requires honing skills that come from the experience of trial and error. This book progresses methodically from understanding the terminology, tools, and making of basic cheeses before moving on to the making of more advanced styles of cheeses.

In **Part 1, "The Composition of Cheese,"** you will learn the physical composition of cheese, all about milk and starter cultures used for cheese making, and the tools required.

In **Part 2, "Making Quick Cheeses,"** you will embark on making fresh cheeses by the direct-acidification method, including paneer, mozzarella, and crème fraîche. You will also learn how to use cheesecloth and make culture-ripened fresh cheeses.

Part 3, "Cultured Cheese and Conventional Cheese Making," details the formal cheese-making process step by step and moves into more advanced cheese making, including hard and brined cheeses such as cheddar and Baby Swiss.

Sidebars

Helpful and interesting information is provided throughout the book in sidebars to assist you in learning about cheese and the making of cheese.

Cheese Bite

Tips and helpful hints about cheeses and the process of making them.

Whey Watch

Things to avoid or be cautious of when making cheese.

def•i•ni•tion

Cheese-making terms and tools explained.

Tasty Chatter

Interesting facts and information about the world of cheese.

Acknowledgments

I must thank my wife Eileen and all of the Leeners staff for picking up the workload and filling in for me and others as I diverted resources, leaving them shorthanded. A special thank you goes to Joellen Ionni for her hours spent in our test kitchen perfecting the recipes and techniques used in this book. This project could not have been accomplished without her assistance. I wish to thank Carol Jenkins for monitoring my literary voice and helping to translate my sometimes random thoughts into coherent sentences; and my assistant Crystal Wisniewski, who acted as coordinator, researcher, and proofreader.

I must also mention Peter Dixon, dairy foods consultant and artisan cheesemaker, for his assistance and prompt response to our questions (www.dairyfoodsconsulting.com).

Trademarks

All terms mentioned in this book that are known to be or are suspected of being trademarks or service marks have been appropriately capitalized. Alpha Books and Penguin Group (USA) Inc. cannot attest to the accuracy of this information. Use of a term in this book should not be regarded as affecting the validity of any trademark or service mark.

Part 1

The Composition of Cheese

In order to make cheese, one must have a firm understanding of what a cheese is. We start by looking at cheese from the consumer's perspective and noting the physical characteristics that make individual cheeses unique, identifying different types of cheese and how to recognize the categories where they belong. Next we look at cheese from a technical point of view, identifying the qualities in milk that make it possible for you to turn it into cheese—the ability to select the proper milk for cheese making will be critical to your success.

We also look at cheese with a scientific eye to understand cheese making as a biological and chemical process. You will learn about the agents and additives used to create the chemical reactions needed to transform milk into cheese.

A Meeting with the Big Cheese

In This Chapter

- The anatomy of cheese
- The three classifications of cheese in cheesemaker's terms
- How to define the cheese you are making

To make a cheese, it is important to first understand what a cheese is by definition and composition. We will explore both of these elements in this chapter, in order to give you the knowledge needed to understand the process of cheese making later on. While you will not actually make a cheese in this chapter, you will learn valuable information and establish a foundation of knowledge that will benefit you greatly throughout the book.

Cheese is a food composed of the coagulated protein and fat in the milk collected from dairy animals. The actual invention of cheese as we know it today evolved over centuries of discovery brought about by circumstance, or what I call good luck. It has been a long journey from that first bowl of curdled milk to the unique flavor and texture of nine-year-old cheddar. Leaving history to culinary historians, we will stay focused on making cheese in your kitchen.

The Anatomy of a Cheese

Your interest in this book says that you've probably spent some time around the cheese counter at the local market. Our goal in this chapter is to establish a common ground in terms of what you already know about cheese and the knowledge needed to make it. The best place to start is with the physical characteristics of popular cheeses. The following illustration of common cheese attributes will be your road map to the terms and descriptions used throughout the book.

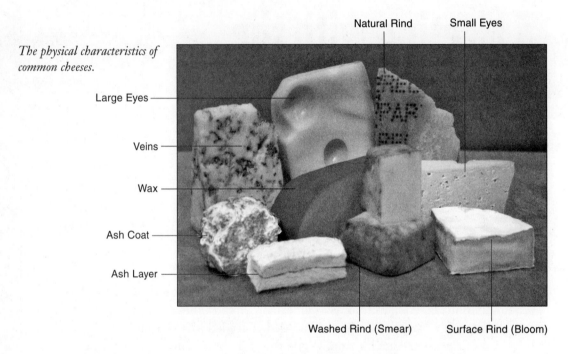

The physical characteristics of common cheeses.

The following are the physical attributes of cheeses:

Ash Coat: Many goat cheeses are covered with a fine coating of food-grade ash made from activated charcoal. The ash is tasteless and is used to reduce the acidity of the cheese surface. This promotes the growth of favorable surface molds which provide complex flavor compounds. Ash-coated cheese will have a milder flavor than the same cheese made without the coating. Examples: Valençay (France), Fog Lights Chèvre (United States).

Ash Layer: Traditionally, a light layer of ash is applied to the top of fresh-made goat or sheep milk cheeses as they are placed into molds. This edible line separates cheese made from different batches of milk. The ash provides the same acid-reducing effect as an ash coat, creating a cheese with a milder interior flavor. An ash coat may also be applied at the cheesemaker's discretion. Examples: Morbier (France), Humboldt Fog Chèvre (United States).

Surface Rind (Bloom): The encouragement of richly flavorful molds on cheese during a brief aging process also creates structural integrity, allowing a solid cheese to contain a soft, almost fluid interior. Cheesemakers refer to this as bloomy rind or mold-ripened cheese. Examples: Camembert (France), Brie (France).

Large Eyes: The large holes found in some Alpine-style cheeses are formed as the cheese ages in a very controlled environment. The holes, called eyes, are caused by the interior production of carbon dioxide gas. The method used to produce the gas also provides the distinctive flavor exhibited by these cheeses. Examples: Emmental (Switzerland), Jarlsberg (Norway).

Small Eyes: Cheeses that show small gaps in their interiors are said to have small eyes. These develop in the same way as large eyes, but the amount of carbon dioxide produced is limited. Small eyes give the cheese a lighter texture while maintaining its structural integrity. Examples: Havarti (Denmark), Baby Swiss (United States).

> **Cheese Bite**
>
> An experienced cheesemaker can assess the quality of a Swiss cheese simply by looking into its eyes. Their size, shape, and uniformity will be a warning about problems that occurred during production.

Natural Rind: This distinctive armorlike coating develops on cheeses that are aged for weeks rather than days. Natural rind cheeses can appear to be wrapped in unfinished leather or stone. The aroma can be pungent and strong. Eating the actual natural rind is a matter of personal taste, but the protected cheese inside is complex and full of character. Examples: Tomme de Savoie (France), Stilton (England).

Washed Rind (Smear): Washing the rind is the process of a cheese being wiped (washed) with a salted liquid prior to aging. The liquids used range from water to beer and wine. The wash is applied to promote the even growth of desirable surface microorganisms. The washing liquid is smeared evenly over the entire cheese, resulting in a smear coat. The process also distributes the microorganisms over the cheese.

In some cases the washing liquid breaks down the surface of the cheese and the rind, then becomes part of the cheese rather than just surrounding it. When the character of the liquid used is transferred to the cheese, in some cases it complements the creamy smooth interior and in other cases it provides a sharp contrast. Examples: Taleggio (Italy), Mahon (Spain), Trappist-style cheeses.

Tasty Chatter

The Trappist monks of Chimay in Belgium brew some of the world's most extraordinary beers, which they also use to produce unique and exceptional cheeses. Using their beer to wash the cheese creates a recognizable bond between the two. The beer helps the natural rind develop and lends a surprisingly mild beer flavor to a cheese whose aroma can be best described as aggressive.

Wax: Pliable food-grade wax is traditionally used to seal cheese and protect it from air and humidity while maintaining the desired moisture content. The wax is flexible enough to expand and contract with the cheese without cracking. Colored waxes have become associated with particular cheeses, most notably red-waxed Gouda, but there are no hard-and-fast rules for selecting a wax color. In general, black wax is used for cheeses that are aged for longer periods. Red wax is applied to milder cheeses, and brown can represent smoked cheese. Each cheesemaker will have his or her reasons for selecting one over the other. Examples: Gouda (Holland), cheddar (United States).

Veins: Veining of the cheese interior is most recognizable in blue cheese. The veins are produced by exposing the interior of the cheese to the air. This is accomplished by "spiking" the cheese prior to aging. Holes are poked through the cheese and these "tunnels" become the main vein as blue mold grows on the walls. Additional veins may branch off in all directions depending on the condition of the curd. The mold produces the unmistakable aroma and flavors associated with these cheeses. Examples: Roquefort (France), Gorgonzola (Italy).

Classifications of Cheese

It is important to be able to identify the type of cheese you make in terms of the classifications recognized by cheesemakers and consumers everywhere. The general classifications defined by *The American Cheese Society* are specialty cheese, artisan cheese, and farmstead cheese. Your homemade cheese may or may not fall into one of these classifications, and a single cheese can easily fall into more than one classification.

When reading the label of a cheese at the store or market, check for one of these classifications. In most cases, the class with the most emphasis placed on it will be the one that is deemed by the cheesemaker to be most important in accurately representing their

def•i•ni•tion

The American Cheese Society is a nonprofit member organization, based in Louisville, Kentucky, that provides consumer guidelines and definitions of different cheese classifications, as well as education and resources for cheesemakers.

product. For example, a cheese produced using the milk from the cheesemaker's cows and using traditional methods may be called artisanal farmstead cheese—placing the emphasis on the process rather than the milk source.

Specialty Cheese

Specialty cheese is defined as a cheese of limited production, with particular attention paid to the natural flavor and texture profiles. Specialty cheeses may be made from all types of milk (cow, sheep, and goat) and may include flavorings such as herbs, spices, fruits, and nuts.

Artisan Cheese

The word *artisan* or *artisanal* implies that a cheese is produced primarily by hand, in small batches, with particular attention paid to the tradition of the cheesemaker's art, and using as little mechanization as possible in the production of the cheese. Artisan cheeses may be made from all types of milk and may include various flavorings. Artisan cheeses can be found in quality cheese shops and many grocery stores that showcase local cheesemakers.

Farmstead Cheese

In order for a cheese to be classified as "farmstead," as defined by The American Cheese Society, the cheese must be made with milk from the cheesemaker's own herd, or flock, on the farm where the animals are raised. Milk used in the production of farmstead cheeses may not be obtained from any outside source. Farmstead cheeses may be made from all types of milk and may include various flavorings.

Farmstead cheeses are often available at rural farmers' markets, especially in areas of Amish and Mennonite communities. Some cheese shops and grocery stores may also carry local farmstead cheeses.

What Kind of Cheese Will You Make?

If you use milk from your own dairy animals, you will very likely be able to identify your cheese as farmstead. Most of the recipes in this book use very traditional cheese-making techniques and therefore may be considered as artisan. Those recipes that step outside these traditions are denoted by the word "style" in the recipe title, such as "mozzarella-style cheese." Since the majority of readers will be using milk purchased from the grocery store, all of the cheese recipes in this book are classified as home-made, and no claims can be made about them other than that.

Categories of Cheese

Once classified, cheeses can then be placed into categories. Categories generally describe the style in which a cheese is produced. The categories used by cheesemakers are: fresh, soft-ripened, semi-soft, hard, blue, pasta filata, natural rind, washed rind, and processed. These terms are also familiar to most cheese lovers and are commonly used to help consumers identify the type of cheese they are buying. The names are important to the home cheesemaker because they tell us much about how the cheese is made and whether or not there are special ingredients or processes needed to produce it.

The following information provides the general definitions and unique characteristics of each cheese category. In the list of cheese examples for each category, those in bold print have recipes in this book.

Fresh Cheese

Fresh cheese is used to describe cheeses that have not been aged at all, or are very slightly cured. These cheeses have high moisture content. They are usually creamy and mild in flavor with a soft texture. All types of milk are used and in the United States, by law, the milk must be pasteurized. Examples of fresh cheeses are **mascarpone, ricotta, chèvre,** cream cheese, quark, **cottage cheese, yogurt cheese, queso blanco, paneer,** and **queso fresco.**

> **Cheese Bite**
>
> Buy it, then eat it. It is always best to consume fresh cheeses before the expiration date indicated on the package, as they are highly perishable. Fresh cheese, like wine, is only sold once it is ready to be consumed.

Many fresh cheeses will have multiple classifications, and some will include all three. An herb-coated chèvre produced on a goat farm using the traditional methods of production can be considered a specialty artisanal farmstead fresh cheese.

Semi-Soft Cheese

Semi-soft cheeses have a smooth, creamy interior with little or no rind. They are generally high in moisture content and range from very mild in flavor to very pungent. These cheeses can be made from any dairy milk, either pasteurized or raw depending on the aging requirements and the desired style. Examples of semi-soft cheeses include blue cheeses, **Colby,** Fontina styles, **Havarti, Monterey Jack,** and **farmhouse cheddar.**

Soft-Ripened Cheese

Soft-ripened describes cheeses which are *ripened* from the outside in. This ripening is accomplished by inoculating the milk or spraying the surface of the cheese with a mold called *Penicillium candidum.* This mold forms an edible rind that encases the complete cheese during a brief aging time. This type of rind is called bloom and can appear white or white with red and brown flecks. Most notably, soft-ripened cheeses have very soft centers that become runny when warmed, as in baked Brie. Examples of soft-ripened cheeses include Brie, Camembert, and triple crèmes.

def•i•ni•tion

Ripening refers to a process in which cheese is stored under conditions that promote the surface growth of beneficial bacteria to produce specific flavors, aromas, and textures.

Hard Cheese

The terms "hard" and "firm" are used to describe a very broad spectrum of cheeses with taste profiles ranging from very mild to sharp and pungent. The range of textures is equally as broad, going from soft and pliable at room temperature to so hard that the cheese needs to be grated. These cheeses may be made from any dairy milk, pasteurized or not. The type of milk used will depend on the cheese being produced and the cheesemaker's preference. Examples of hard cheeses are **Gouda,** most **traditional cheddars,** Swiss, Gruyère, Parmesan, and **Baby Swiss.**

Blue Cheese

Blue describes cheeses that have a distinctive blue-green veining and the distinctive aroma and flavor created by the *Penicillium roqueforti* mold. The mold is added directly to the cheese milk or is layered into the curds as the cheese shape is being formed. Growth of the blue mold is activated by the spiking method described earlier in the chapter. The aroma and flavor that this mold adds to the cheese ranges from fairly mild to assertive and pungent. Blue cheeses can be found within all of the other cheese categories and may be produced from pasteurized or raw milk, depending on the aging time of the cheese. Examples of blue cheeses include French Roquefort, Italian Gorgonzola, Danish blue, and English Stilton.

Pasta Filata Cheese

Assigned to a whole family of Italian-style cheeses, pasta filata is Italian for "spun paste," which describes the unique process of kneading and stretching the curds. In English, these cheeses are called stretched curd or pulled curd. Cheeses in this category can be placed in any of the classifications, from fresh to hard grating cheese. Examples of pasta filata cheeses are **mozzarella, provolone,** and scamorza.

Natural and Washed Rind Cheeses

Natural rind cheeses have natural rinds that develop during the aging process without the addition of *molds* or *microflora* as with soft-ripened cheese. The necessary molds and microflora must appear naturally from the environment. These cheeses are also not washed with any agent used to create an exterior rind. Natural rind cheeses are usually made from unpasteurized raw milk, which is possible because of the extended aging time needed for the rind and flavors to develop. Examples of natural cheeses include French Tomme de Savoie and mimolette, English Stilton (which is also a blue), and Lancashire.

def•i•ni•tion

The **molds** and **microflora** used in cheese making are actually microscopic organisms that are safe to eat. They produce distinctive aromas and flavors on their own, as well as through interaction with the cheese. The most recognized of these is *Penicillium roqueforti,* found in blue cheese. It is not unusual for multiple strains to be used in a single cheese. This is often done when a secondary organism creates or improves the environment for the primary organism.

Washed rind cheeses are those that are surface-ripened by washing the cheese throughout the ripening and aging process. The wash liquid can be salt brine, beer, wine, brandy, or a mixture of ingredients that encourage the growth of bacteria. The rind that develops has a bright orange to brown appearance. The flavors and aromas of these cheeses are quite pungent, yet the texture is often semi-soft to creamy. Pasteurized or raw milk may be used depending on the style being made and the cheesemaker's preference. Examples of washed rind cheeses are triple-crème and semi-soft cheeses similar to Epoisses, Livarot, and Taleggio.

Processed Cheese Products

Processed cheeses are by-product foods made from a combination of natural cheese and other ingredients such as stabilizers (sodium citrate and sodium phosphate), emulsifiers (carageenan and Xanthan gum), and flavor enhancers (cheese-flavored substances that are either natural or artificial). The aims of these added ingredients are consistency and extended shelf life—a requirement of mass-market consumption. Examples are American cheese, processed cheese spreads, and "cheese flavored" spreads.

The United States Department of Agriculture (USDA) has also established very specific definitions for individual types and styles of cheese. These are most important to consumers who rely on the names and descriptions of cheeses as they appear on package labels. The guidelines also help producers classify the cheese they are selling and may be used by the home cheesemaker when there is a question regarding how a specific cheese is produced. A free handbook of cheese names and descriptions published by the USDA is available online at http://naldr.nal.usda.gov/NALWeb/ Agricola_Link.asp?Accession=CAT87210559. Also see Appendix B for this and additional links.

Be the Cheese

Like your first whiff of a fresh Limburger cheese, all this information can be overwhelming at first. There's no need to memorize everything you have read here; it is here so that you can easily refer back to it as you move through the book and increase your cheese-making knowledge and experience.

Throughout this book, the names of cheeses and a recipe for any given cheese are considered loose homemade representations of cheese styles. Your homemade cheese will have the flavor and character of its namesake cheese, and you will use methods as close to the artisan style as can be managed in your kitchen. You can decide if your cheese meets any of the established requirements for other claims. It takes practice to become good at anything, so remember to have fun and enjoy your experience of cheese making.

The Least You Need to Know

- The physical attributes of a cheese, such as the size of eyes or the texture of the rind, tell the story of how a cheese was made.

- The three classifications of cheese, as established by The American Cheese Society and recognized by cheesemakers and consumers, are specialty, artisan, and farmstead.

- Several categories of cheese define a cheese by the style in which it was produced.

Chapter 2

Where Cheese Comes From

In This Chapter

- ♦ Looking at cheese from a scientific perspective
- ♦ Milk as the primary component of cheese
- ♦ Finding the right milk for the hobby cheesemaker
- ♦ The science of protein manipulation
- ♦ The contributions of salt to cheese making

It is time to "cut the cheese" so to speak and take a look inside the composition of cheese. In the simplest definition, there are only four ingredients needed to produce cheese. The list is topped by milk. The physical properties of dairy milk are what make cheese possible. Cheese milk (milk selected and prepared for cheese making) is the source of the physical appearance, flavors, and aromas described in Chapter 1. In this chapter, we will break down the generality of cheese into the chemical composition of its base material and explain the microscopic tools used by cheesemakers to extract solid cheese from liquid milk.

What Is Cheese?

Cheese is made from milk that has come from traditional domesticated dairy animals including cows, goats, and sheep. Cheese may also be made from a blend of the milks from these animals. Outside of America, the use of milk from more exotic animals like water buffalo and yak is common. Regardless of the source, what makes milk into cheese is the removal of a large portion of the water. This is accomplished through a variety of means, ranging from chemical additions to mechanical processing.

If you are lucky enough to have an Italian import store or a quality cheese shop close by, familiarize yourself with the same cheese made from the milk of different species. The best way to do this is to prepare a cheese-tasting session for family and friends using American-style mozzarella (partly skim), imported fresh buffalo mozzarella, and if possible, a mozzarella made from goat's milk. You may find additional variations of mozzarella to include as well.

Right away you are going to notice major differences in the packaging. Some will be in the usual vacuum-packed plastic; others will be floating in tubs of water or brine—these are the fresh versions of the cheese and require the brine to prevent spoilage for a very short period of time. Take notes as you taste each cheese, recording the texture, how long the salt remains present, your sense of the milk flavor, and your overall impressions. Your notes will become a valuable reference as you begin to evaluate your own cheeses.

Tasty Chatter

A bison is not a buffalo. In America, the word buffalo is used interchangeably with bison; however, they are two different animals. Both are from the Bovidae family, but the buffalo species is native to Africa and Asia. By Italian law, mozzarella may only be made from water buffalo milk which contains up to 16 percent milkfat, as compared to 4 percent from other breeds of buffalo.

There is great variability among different dairy breeds within the same species. The milk from a certain breed of cow is often preferred by individual cheesemakers for specific cheeses. The significant factor for the cheesemaker is the ratio of fat to protein. Table 2.1 shows the difference in fat and protein between breeds. These differences account for regional variations in the flavor and texture of the same cheese style. This is also true of dairy products sold by competing creameries in the same region. For example, milk from Jersey cows is preferred for butter production because of its high fat content.

Table 2.1: Intra-Species Percentage Composition of Milk

Cow Breed	Water	Fat	Protein	Lactose	Ash*
Holstein	87.74	3.40	3.22	4.87	0.68
Brown Swiss	86.59	4.01	3.61	5.04	0.73
Guernsey	85.39	4.95	3.91	4.93	0.74
Jersey	85.09	5.37	3.92	4.93	0.71
Buffalo**	83.63	6.56	3.88	5.23	0.70

Ash is the term used to describe the collection of minerals found in milk—predominantly potassium, calcium, and phosphorus.

**Murrah buffalo is the primary milking breed of buffalo herded in Italy, Bulgaria, Egypt, India, and Pakistan, among other countries. Murrah buffalo milk is used to make Italian mozzarella.*

Moisture content is the most recognizable physical characteristic of a cheese. Soft cheese contains more water than hard cheese, giving it a higher moisture content. Very dry cheeses, like Parmesan, contain almost no water. There is a direct relationship between the moisture content of cheese and its shelf life. High moisture cheeses will spoil more quickly because the presence of water makes the environment friendlier to unwanted bacteria when the cheese is exposed to the air. This is true even if the cheese is kept refrigerated. On the other hand, a very dry, well-aged, hard cheese—like the ones you grate over pasta—can be properly stored in the refrigerator for almost a year once it is opened.

Murrah buffalo.

The water is removed from milk during a process called "separation of curds and whey." After separation, what remains is the watery liquid called whey and a collection of solid milk compounds called curds. Whey is the liquid portion of milk composed mostly of water and soluble lactose, with trace amounts of fat, proteins, and minerals.

The curds are what make up a cheese. Curds consist of the milk protein called casein, milkfat (butterfat), lactose (milk sugar), calcium, and other minerals.

Since cheese is essentially concentrated milk, it is a compact powerhouse of nutrition. When cheese is made properly, the result is an all-natural and delicious food source.

Tasty Chatter
Remember Little Miss Muffet "eating her curds and whey"? Miss Muffet's mother was likely a typical Middle Ages housewife who would make a simple dairy product of coagulated milk solids, or curds, which were served with a little of the tart watery liquid, or whey. Centuries later, this dish has evolved into cottage cheese.

Table 2.2: How the Components of Milk Are Proportioned into Curds and Whey During Cheese Making

	Whole Milk		Whey		Cheese	
Water	87.50%	116.20 oz.	94%	109.23 oz.	6%	6.97 oz.
Milkfat	3.20%	4.25 oz.	6%	0.25 oz.	94%	3.99 oz.
Casein	3.55%	4.71 oz.	4%	0.19 oz.	96%	4.53 oz.
Whey Protein*	0.75%	1.00 oz.	96%	0.96 oz.	4%	0.04 oz.
Lactose	5.00%	6.64 oz.	94%	6.24 oz.	6%	0.40 oz.
Total	100.00%	132.80 oz.		116.87 oz.		15.93 oz.
In Pounds		8.30 lb.		7.30 lb.		1.00 lb.

The proteins appearing in the whey after precipitation are collectively called whey proteins.

As you can see in Table 2.2, of the 116.20 ounces of water in whole milk, 94 percent will remain in the whey and 6 percent is carried through to the curd after separation.

Making one cheese different from another is primarily accomplished by two controlling events: the method used to cause separation, and what happens once the curds are formed. The curds can be cut, cooked, washed, squeezed, shrunk, packed, pressed, drained, salted, stirred, soaked … the list seems endless, and we will cover these different processes in a later chapter.

Milk for Cheese Making

As we learned earlier, you can make cheese from any dairy animal's milk. Farm-fresh raw milk as well as many store-bought brands ranging from whole to low fat may be used to make cheese. The first rule of thumb, regardless of the source of your milk, is "the fresher the better." When purchasing milk from a grocery store, check the labeling as well as the freshness dates. If possible, purchase milk supplied by a local dairy. That milk did not have to travel as far to get to your store, so chances are it has not been processed with excessive heat during pasteurization. Don't be afraid to ask your grocer for milk from the latest delivery.

Cheese Bite

Ask your store's dairy manager about his or her milk suppliers. He or she should be familiar with the quality of the milk received and may be able to tell you some of the specifics about the suppliers' processing methods. You may also find useful information on the milk producer's website. A website or at least a toll-free telephone number should appear on the carton. As always, milk should be kept refrigerated until needed.

Homogenized milk is an emulsified colloid of fat and water, meaning the fat and the water are evenly dispersed throughout the milk. In a colloid, two compounds which are considered to be opposites (like oil and water) will remain blended because one compound is evenly dispersed within the other. Homogenizing is a process in which the milkfat or cream molecules are mechanically broken up into microscopic particles so they can mix evenly with the water. This is done to prevent the cream from separating out of the milk and collecting at the top. There may be local dairies which offer your store milk that is not homogenized. This is called cream-line or cream-top milk and can be identified by the cream that naturally rises to the top of the container. If available, this type of milk is preferred over homogenized because it will form a firmer curd.

Cheese Bite

An emulsion, as opposed to an emulsified colloid, is a substance comprised of two compounds that will naturally separate from each other but are held together by a third molecule which has the ability to attach to fat at one end and water at the other.

All raw milk, regardless of its source, will naturally contain both beneficial and pathogenic bacteria. Pasteurization is a heat process designed to kill all bacteria that may be present in the raw milk. Pasteurization may also extend the shelf life of milk by killing the organisms and deactivating the enzymes that can cause milk to spoil more quickly. This process has been in use in the United States since the 1900s due to the increased distribution of milk for sale to areas far removed from the farm. It is safe to say that all store-bought milk will be pasteurized.

There are different methods of pasteurization for dairy milk. Vat or bulk pasteurization is where a large volume of milk is heated in a large vessel. Flash pasteurization is where a small amount of milk is heated and cooled very quickly as it travels through a thin tube. The minimum processing temperatures and times to pasteurize are 145°F for 30 minutes for vat pasteurization and 161°F for 15 seconds for high-temperature flash pasteurization. Milk that has been pasteurized in this way will work very well for the home cheesemaker.

The pasteurization methods, temperatures, and times described previously were the norm until recently. Around 2004, some larger national and even regional dairies increased their pasteurization temperatures to above 170°F. The reasons for this are not totally clear, and the discovery was made when I began receiving calls for help getting homemade mozzarella to stretch. Since the recipe had not changed, it had to be the milk. (I came to this conclusion after noticing that all the calls were coming from localized parts of the country. Further investigation pointed to the same dairy processor.) Milk which is heated to 170°F may give less than satisfactory results in cheese making because the protein becomes so *denatured* that it does not respond as expected to standard cheese-making methods. This is all the more reason to source your milk from a local dairy. It is a good idea to get to know your local dairy supplier, so that you know who to call if you run into problems or have questions.

def•i•ni•tion

In cheese making, **denatured** refers to the permanent altered state of milk protein molecules caused by exposure to excessive heat. This means that once treated by high-temperature pasteurization, the protein will not necessarily react "naturally" during the cheese-making process. The most notable result is that the curd will hold onto more of the whey, resulting in a weaker curd (one that falls apart) and cheese with higher than normal moisture.

There is also a class of dairy products—including milk—that are called "ultra-pasteurized." This means the milk is heated to 280°F for two seconds. This is done to increase the shelf life of milk that has to travel longer distances for distribution or milk that will remain on store shelves longer due to price or demand. Many organic milk brands and most specialty milks like goat's milk fall into this category. This may seem counterintuitive when considering the best quality of milk for your cheese making. Organic dairy products have increased in popularity and availability, but for cheese making they just won't work once they have been ultrapasteurized. Make certain that the milk you purchase for cheese making is not labeled ultrapasteurized (by law, it must be labeled if it is), as this type of milk will not form a curd.

There are a number of online resources to help you locate the milk most suitable for home cheese making. For instance, www.smalldairy.com provides a listing of small dairy farms by region and what type of products they sell. Additional resources are provided in Appendix B.

One of the main differences between using nonhomogenized, vat-pasteurized milk and many store-bought brands is the quality of the curd. When using minimally processed milk, it is more apparent when the curd is ready for processing. The result-ing curd is also firmer and more resilient. It will withstand the subsequent steps in cheese making better than overprocessed milk.

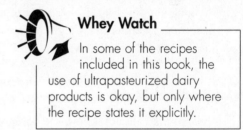

Whey Watch

In some of the recipes included in this book, the use of ultrapasteurized dairy products is okay, but only where the recipe states it explicitly.

Another easily recognizable difference is the color of the resulting cheese. Minimally processed milk may come from cows that pasture graze. Their milk will be higher in beta-carotene, vitamin A, and vitamin E. These produce a cheese with a deeper yellow color. Conversely, most store-bought milk comes from cows with diets higher in grain and will result in a whiter appearance.

Using Store-Bought Milk

When the appropriate industrially pasteurized milk is used, the home cheesemaker must still compensate for the altered protein. Without adjustment, the milk will not respond properly and the curd will remain too soft. Compensating for this is not diffi-cult. The addition of a 30 percent solution of calcium chloride at the rate of not more than ½ teaspoon per gallon will do the trick. The addition will help adjust for the over processing of store-bought milk in two ways. It contributes extra calcium ions and slightly increases the acidity of the milk. Both of these factors result in a firmer curd being formed and in less time. Specific instructions for using calcium chloride are given in each of our recipes.

Do not be tempted to run out to the garage and weigh out a handful of the calcium chloride you use to melt the ice on your driveway. It is definitely not edible. Only pharmaceutical-grade chemicals can be used in cheese making. It is also necessary that the calcium chloride be in a 30 percent solution. It cannot be added in dry form directly to the milk. The reason is in the chemical reaction caused by rehydration of the compound—it gets hot, surprisingly hot!

A 30 percent solution indicates that 30 percent of the total, by weight, is pharmaceutical-grade calcium chloride and 70 percent is distilled water. The correct solution can be purchased ready-to-use from suppliers online. If you are unable to locate a supplier, you should be able to find the raw materials at a beer- and wine-making supply shop. If you are attempting to make your own solution, it is very important to measure weight (not volume) and use pharmaceutical-grade calcium chloride with distilled water.

Using Raw Milk

As you may already know, the composition of raw milk will vary with the seasons, the diet and health of the animal, and even the time of day the animal is milked. There are also distinct differences between species. For example, goat's milk will produce a much thinner or looser curd than cow's milk. This is very evident in goat milk yogurt, which is almost runny, whereas cow's milk yogurt can be as firm as gelatin. One difference between the two raw milks is that goat's milk is naturally homogenized. The fat will not easily separate out. Using milk from a different species in a recipe calling for milk from one specific species will require adjustments ranging from the amount of ingredients required to the ingredients themselves, not to mention changes to the actual process. These modifications can be extensive. It is best to locate a recipe from a trusted source that calls for the type of milk you will be using, rather than going it alone.

Tasty Chatter

My Great Aunt Liza owned a small dairy farm with a herd of about 12 cows. At certain times of the growing season, Aunt Liza's cows liked to eat horseradish plants. Anyone who has ever made home-prepared horseradish root can attest to the effects it has on the respiratory system—burning eyes, runny nose, shortness of breath. When milking the cows, you can imagine the effects of a cow's all-day consumption of raw horseradish tops on the milker. The horseradish not only caused bad breath; it also tainted the milk.

In cheese making, just like cooking, "raw" means unprocessed, and with milk it specifically means unpasteurized. Many states have outlawed the sale of raw milk directly to the public. An alternative way to purchase raw milk is to purchase a herd share. With a herd share program, you pay the dairy farmer to board, care for, and milk your cow or goat. You are then responsible for collecting your share of the milk produced. Details of a herd share program can be found at www.realmilk.com/cowfarmshare.html. Additional sources of milk availability are given in Appendix B.

If you have access to raw milk from cows, sheep, or goats, we encourage you to use it, but there are some rules. By law, in the United States and many other countries, any cheese made for sale that will not be aged for more than 60 days must be produced with pasteurized milk. Aging beyond 60 days provides time for any harmful bacteria to basically die off. This comes about mostly due to the environment becoming inhospitable to them. Failure to permit time for this to occur can result in serious infectious diseases, including listeriosis and salmonellosis among others. There is significant debate among artisan cheesemakers over the validity of this law, and even more debate among cheese connoisseurs over the quality and flavor of fresh cheeses made with raw versus pasteurized milk. Given the health risks, keep in mind this is nothing for the amateur to be playing around with.

Whey Watch

If you are using raw milk, pasteurizing is recommended in order to kill any pathogenic bacteria that may be present. If you choose not to pasteurize your raw milk, the cheese produced must be aged over 60 days in order for the aging process to take care of killing off unwanted bacteria.

The use of indirect heat via a water bath will prevent the milk from scalding. Stir frequently until the temperature of the milk reaches 161°F. Hold milk at 161°F for a minimum of 15 seconds, after which the milk must be cooled quickly and refrigerated or, if making cheese immediately, cooled to the inoculation temperature in the cheese recipe.

Cheeses which are aged for more than 60 days may be made with either pasteurized or raw milk. On the other hand, cheeses in the natural rind category are professionally made with raw milk. It is strongly recommended that the inexperienced home or farmstead cheesemaker pasteurize as part of the cheese-making process whenever raw milk is involved.

Although you will be performing the pasteurization in a manner suited to cheese making, you may also need to add a certain amount of calcium chloride, as described previously. You will need to experiment a little to adjust each recipe. Try the recipes included in this book as they are written, then make adjustments as needed. Details on adjusting milk for cheese making are given in Chapter 7.

Many of the descriptions of the transitional states of milk during cheese making are based on observations made when nonhomogenized raw milk is low-temperature pasteurized and used immediately.

Using Powdered Milk

If you are unable to purchase milk that is not ultrapasteurized, or you are having difficulty forming a good curd with the milk in your area, powdered milk may be an alternative. There are three different heat treatments that nonfat dry milk can receive, and only one works for cheese making.

High-heat treatment consists of spray drying pasteurized skim milk at a temperature of 190°F for 30 minutes. Medium-heat treatment is 160°F to 175°F for 20 minutes. Low-heat treatment is not more than 160°F for 2 minutes, which is what is used for cheese.

High- and medium-heat-treated dry milk is made primarily for use in the manufacture of other foods. It can be found in products ranging from baked goods and processed meats to dry mixes and ice cream. Just like regular milk that has been pasteurized at high temperatures, it is not suitable for cheese making.

Most nonfat dry milk for sale to consumers is processed by low-heat treatment, so it should retain enough undenatured protein to coagulate in cheese making. When replacing whole milk with powdered, reconstitute enough nonfat dry milk to make 7 pints of milk according to the manufacturer's directions. Add 1 pint of heavy cream (preferred), coffee cream, or half-and-half (ultrapasteurized is okay in this case because it represents a small amount in the whole gallon of milk). This type of milk will also benefit from the addition of calcium chloride to improve curd firmness. Additional preparation may be necessary based on the cheese being made. There will be a noticeable difference in flavor and quality of cheese made from nonfat dry milk versus raw or fresh milk; however, the addition of cream will improve flavor as well as increase yield compared to cheese made with straight nonfat milk.

Cheese Bite

Instant nonfat dry milk granules do not last forever. An opened container can be stored in a cool, dry place for about three months if it is kept tightly sealed. Once reconstituted, the milk must be stored and handled like fresh milk.

Although nonfat dry milk is made from pasteurized milk, it is not considered sterile. During the process that extracts the water, creating dry granules, it is possible that an acceptable amount of bacteria, including coliforms, are introduced. Coliforms are a class of bacteria that includes *E. coli*, and *E. coli* has an appetite for lactose.

These allowable bacterial levels are minute and of no concern when dry milk is prepared as directed and handled as if it were fresh milk. Once reconstituted, however, cheese and yogurt making is not an intended use. Making cheese and yogurt requires that the milk spend a period of time in the temperature range called the "danger zone." Under these conditions, there exists the potential for these unwanted bacteria to take hold, but it is highly unlikely. When dry milk is used in cheese or yogurt, it should be reconstituted and then heated to 145°F and held there for 30 minutes. Better safe than sorry!

Whey Watch

Nonfat dry milk cannot be considered sterile and must be pasteurized prior to use in cheese or yogurt.

Powdered milk made from milk other than cow's milk is available in some markets and online. It is very tempting to use powdered goat's milk to produce a real goat's milk cheese, for example. The results will almost always be disappointing and in no way will they do justice to the real thing. The use of powdered milk from animals other than cows is not recommended.

What Is Important About the Milk

Throughout this book when you see the word milk, this is referring to store-bought, pasteurized, and homogenized whole cow's milk. In cases where another type of milk or dairy product is called for, it is indicated as such, as in "goat's milk" or "half-and-half," for example. If the milk of different species are interchangeable in a recipe, that will also be noted. Where these distinctions are not made, stick to the recipe as closely as possible.

One final point about milk for cheese making is that all of the recipes and methods taught in this book are built on the premise that the reason for making the cheese is to preserve the nutritional content of whole milk for consumption later. If you are intent on making low- or no-fat cheese,

Cheese Bite

Dairy farmers refer to the unwanted character of milk resulting from an animal's diet as "feed and weed" flavors.

salt-free cheese, lactose-free cheese, or anything called a processed cheese product, this is not the book for you. While these foods do exist in the marketplace and serve as a satisfying substitute for those people who use them, their production requirements are far beyond the scope of the home cheesemaker.

Cheese Starter Cultures

We will now look into the microscopic world and examine the chemical and biological agents used to transform milk into cheese. It is true that cheese, like wine, occurs spontaneously in nature. A grape left on the kitchen counter for a month will turn to wine. A bowl of milk left in the sun for a day or two will curdle, making curds and whey. Both are the results of fermentation, and fermentation is the first step in the ultimate process of recycling called decay.

The job of the cheesemaker or winemaker is to control this process, with the goal of avoiding spoilage and making the results the absolute best they can be. They each utilize biological and chemical agents to promote the transformation of raw material into the desired product. Thus begins the exploration into the secrets of the art of cheese making.

In the good old days, starter cultures, or microorganisms, were unknown to both cooks and science. These beneficial bugs were introduced to fresh milk directly from the animal or from the surrounding air in much the same way as sourdough bread yeasts are today. A portion of milk would be left in a warm place overnight to "sour," then used the next day to start a batch of cheese. The problem with this method is that along with the good bacteria, soured milk inevitably contains bad bacteria as well. Please do not be tempted to try one of the pre–Louis Pasteur methods of cheese making. The results could make you and others very sick.

Tasty Chatter
Prior to the discovery of the important role that microorganisms play in producing many foods, the results they produced were often attributed to mysterious forces. For example, brewers would set aside a portion of freshly made unfermented beer, called wort, as an offering to the angels. The next day they would find evidence of the angels' visit and satisfaction, manifested as froth floating on the wort. This bacteria-rich foam was then added to the full brew and the production of alcohol was underway.

In today's world, the standard practice is to inoculate cheese milk with specific cultures to ensure consistent quality. It is just as important for the home cheesemaker to obtain pure cultures and handle them properly to limit the number of possible sources of contamination.

The bacterial cultures used in cheese making are commonly called "starters." This term probably stems from the fact that almost every cheese-making recipe starts with the addition of a lactic acid, producing bacteria in the milk.

There are two primary types of bacterial cultures used in cheese production. They are commonly called mesophilic and thermophilic, yet these terms describe attributes of the bacteria used not the actual cultures. As it pertains to cheese, the word mesophilic generically refers to any lactose-loving organisms that thrive at moderate temperatures in the 77°F to 86°F range. Thermophilic organisms generally prefer temperatures in the 95°F to 105°F range. This distinction is important to the cheese-maker when assessing the requirements of a recipe or selecting a starter for a particular style of cheese.

> **Whey Watch** ___
> When in doubt, if any step in the cheese recipe process (after the addition of the starter) requires that the milk or curd be heated to above 102°F, a thermophilic culture is most likely called for.

Lactic Acid Producing Bacteria

Certain bacteria are responsible for starting the transformation of milk to cheese, and these are in the *Lactococcus* order of the *Streptococcaceae* family. These particular bacteria are the microscopic organisms whose function in cheese making is the controlled production of natural acidity in milk. In the most elementary of terms, these bacteria consume the milk sugar (lactose) and produce lactic acid and other compounds that create the many textures, flavors, and aromas in cheese.

Starter cultures can be single strains of the bacteria or can be used in combinations, depending on the desired character of the finished cheese (see Table 2.3). One classic combination is *Streptococcus thermophilus* and *Lactobacillus helveticus* used together to increase the speed with which lactic acid is produced. This combination is used in many Italian cheeses such as Parmesan and Romano, and Alpine cheeses made in the Emmenthaler and Gruyère styles.

> **Cheese Bite** ___
> Naturally occurring, lactic acid producing bacteria are also used to produce dill pickles and sauerkraut.

Table 2.3: Common Cheeses and the Starter Cultures Used to Produce Them

Popular Cheese Styles	Primary Starter Culture
Cheddar, Colby, cottage	*Lactococcus lactis* ssp. *lactis,* *Lactococcus lactis* ssp. *cremoris*
Cream cheese, Gouda, Camembert	*Lactococcus lactis* ssp. *lactis,* *cremoris,* and *biovar diacetylactis*
Provolone, Swiss	*Streptococcus thermophilus*
Yogurt	*Lactobacillus delbrueckii* ssp. *bulgaricus* with *Streptococcus thermophilus*
Parmesan, Emmenthaler	*Streptococcus thermophilus* with *Lactobacillus helveticus*

ssp. denotes subspecies.

The acidification of milk in cheese making by means of bacteria is called ripening. The bacteria cultures are added to the milk after pasteurization and at specific temperatures. They are allowed to work for specific time periods depending on the type of milk being used and the cheese style to be made. During this period the bacteria begin to consume the milk sugar in the biological process called fermentation.

As the bacteria eat, they produce by-products, including lactic acid, carbon dioxide gas, and other compounds. The presence of lactic acid lowers the pH of the ripening milk. The increasing acidity causes the casein micelles (amino acid chains) to reverse the reaction from polar (repelling each other) to attraction. This change creates a matrix, or microscopic net, that entraps the surrounding milkfat globules along with the bacteria starter and water.

Cheese Bite

Streptococcus lactis is a nonpathogenic species of the *Streptococcus* genus used in cheese making and is not harmful. The closely related *Streptococcus pyogenes* is the pathogenic species known for causing a host of infections, including strep throat. You can safely eat billions of cells of *Streptococcus lactis* in a tablespoon of yogurt, but as few as 1,000 cells of *Streptococcus pyogenes* on an open wound may cause an infection.

The duration of the ripening period will depend on the type of cheese being made. Milk for fresh cheeses that have a longer ripening time will show signs of thickening as the protein gathers up into soft curd. The milk will take on a yogurtlike consistency ranging from thin to firm. This method of milk coagulation is referred to as acid coagulation. The Cultured Yogurt recipe provided later in this chapter will demonstrate it.

Purchasing Cheese Starter Cultures

Shopping for cheese starter cultures can be confusing. Conveniently, cultures are sold as freeze-dried granules much like the packets of bread yeast you find in the grocery store. All too often they are packaged and labeled for the industrial cheese-making market, and this can be intimidating for the home cheesemaker. The label information includes generic names and brand names as well as terms such as single use, recultured, direct set, and direct-to-vat (more on these last two shortly).

When looking at a particular culture, it is best to ignore the given name that may describe a single cheese or cheese style that the culture is intended for. Go directly to the ingredients list and check for the name of the primary culture and any subcultures (ssp.). Compare them to the cultures recommended for the cheese you want to make. If the package listing is generic, try the manufacturer or seller's website to learn what the specific cultures are and compare them to the cultures recommended for your cheese.

All cheese cultures are readily available by mail order and at some beer- and wine-making supply stores. (See Appendix B for a list of sources.)

Direct Set Cultures

In contrast to recultured starters, direct set cultures are products designed to make cheese in a so-called one-step process. These may be called "direct set starters" and are almost always named for the cheese they will make. They will usually be premeasured for a specific, small volume of milk ranging from 1 quart to 1 gallon. Generally, direct set cultures include starter cultures along with other cheese-making enzymes and are not designed for reculturing. Due to the small amount needed, they may also include maltodextrin (a food additive) as carrier or filler. Any combination of starter and enzymes is designed for one-time use and cannot be recultured.

Direct Vat Inoculants

Direct vat inoculants (DVI) cultures have become the most common form of starter used in the cheese industry today. These are also known as direct-to-vat cultures. DVI starters are specific and pure strain cultures and subcultures, without fillers or additives. As the name implies, these cultures are designed to be added directly to milk without any prior preparation. They are manufactured to be quick to activate and perform vigorously, thus reducing the lag phase and preventing mineral precipitation.

DVI cultures have the added advantage of being highly concentrated, meaning that less culture is required to ripen more milk, and lag time is partly addressed by the sheer number of bacterial cells. This translates into a faster and more uniform onset of acid production and better cheese.

To maintain their integrity over time, DVI cultures must be kept frozen. However, even in perfect packaging and storage conditions there are limits. DVIs are meant to be used within their published shelf life to provide maximum acid production.

Prepared Starters

In some older recipes, you will see a call for "prepared starter." The unit of measure will usually be anywhere from 1 tablespoon to 1 cup, depending on the volume of milk. This kitchen volumetric (spoons and cups) reference indicates that the recipe is designed to use a premade culture produced in advance and stored in the refrigerator or freezer. The practice is similar to maintaining a sourdough starter. Preparing a fresh or mother starter involves sterilizing a small batch of milk, cooling it to the appropriate temperature, and then inoculating it with a first-generation, pure-strain starter. The milk is allowed to ripen as the culture reproduces or builds in concentration. The ripened milk can then be stored in the refrigerator for frequent use or divided into individual doses and kept frozen for extended time periods.

Prepared starters that are saved for use at a later date can be problematic, and special attention must be paid to their packaging. Cold storage and freezing will cause the bacteria to become dormant (inactive), thus extending the lag phase when they are added to milk. Lag phase is the period of time between inoculation and the start of fermentation. Extended lag time allows calcium and other minerals to precipitate out of the milk, avoiding capture in the matrix created by the lactic acid.

def•i•ni•tion

Slurry is a concentrated mixture of solids and liquid. In cheese making, it refers to milk that contains a high volume of bacterial cells.

Lag time will be significantly reduced with the use of a cultured *slurry* called a bulk starter. This is prepared by combining the amount of prepared starter needed for the batch with a lesser amount of milk which has been heated to the appropriate temperature. Prepare the slurry a few hours before it is needed. This will give the bacteria time to become fully active.

The use of a prepared starter was widely employed by home and farmstead cheese-makers before the availability of affordable freeze-dried cultures.

What Matters About Cheese Cultures

Most of the recipes in this book that call for a starter use DVI cultures and can be made using *Lactococcus lactis* ssp. *lactis* or *cremoris*, with or without *biovar diacetylactis*. You will recognize it by the generic reference "mesophilic starter." This strain of mesophilic starter is used to make a wide variety of cheeses including soft, semi-hard, and hard cheese. The temperature growth range is 41°F to 100°F with an optimum growth (acid production) range of 77°F to 86°F, making it easy to manage in any kitchen. A few recipes will require other strains of starter to produce both physical characteristics and unique flavors. You will not need to invest in any cultures until you are ready to use them.

Cultured Yogurt

Yogurt is the simplest and possibly the most rewarding of all fermented dairy foods to make. It's a great place to start when learning about cheese making.

In the following recipe for cultured yogurt, you will prepare a batch of active culture yogurt by using an existing starter culture to inoculate milk, which will then demonstrate the effects of acid coagulation.

Ingredients:

1 qt. whole milk suitable for cheese making

1 single-serve container (about 6 oz.) plain yogurt (containing the active bacteria *Lactobacillus bulgaricus* and *Streptococcus thermophilus*; *Lactobacillus acidophilus* may also be included)

Equipment:

Saucepan

Stainless steel bowl large enough to hold at least 1½ qt. and able to sit on top of the saucepan (making a double boiler)

Mixing spoon (not wooden)

Plastic food wrap

Yield: *1 quart*	
Prep time: 12 hours	

1. Turn on the oven light and keep the door closed. The light should provide enough heat to utilize the oven as an incubator. Note that if you are using a gas oven with a constant pilot light, the small flame may be enough to keep the oven warm.

2. Place about 2 inches of water in the saucepan. The water should be shallow and not touch the bottom of the bowl when it is placed over the pan. Put the pan of water on the stove and bring it to a slow boil/simmer. Place the bowl over the simmering water and add the milk.

3. Immediately stir in yogurt. Continue stirring for about 1 minute. The milk should be lukewarm. Do not overheat.

4. Turn off the stove and move the wet bowl to a towel on the countertop. Cover the bowl with plastic food wrap and place it in the oven. Leave the milk in the oven for 12 to 18 hours with the light on. The longer the ripening time, the tangier the yogurt will be.

5. After 12 hours, examine the results. You will see the full effect of coagulation by acidification. The quart of milk has been transformed by controlled fermentation into a second-generation, tart, firm, yogurt curd.

6. The yogurt is now ready to eat! Store it in an airtight container in the refrigerator up to 2 weeks.

Tasty Chatter

Do not get discouraged if you are not successful on your first attempt. Review these possible causes of common problems and try again.

- A pasteurized yogurt was used or the yogurt was out of date.
- The yogurt may have been exposed to extreme heat.
- The milk and yogurt were overheated.
- The oven was not warm enough.

In this Cultured Yogurt recipe, you saw the process of bacteria acidification and experienced the use of a dairy starter culture. The active bacteria in the yogurt were used (recultured) to produce additional yogurt. This process, to an extent, mimics the use of a sourdough starter, where a "sourdough mother" is maintained and drawn out each time bread is made, then replenished or "fed" part of the resulting bread dough.

Reculturing has its limits, however. Each time a culture is reused, it is called a generation. With each generation, there will be many mutations of the original bacteria. Over time, the quality of the finished product will diminish and eventually become unrecognizable. This is very noticeable in the case of yogurt. You will notice that each subsequent generation will become a little more bitter until it becomes undesirable. Even a well-maintained yogurt culture will lose its appeal after about 10 generations. There are those who prefer the taste of a very tart yogurt, but going beyond 17 generations is not recommended. At that point the results cannot really be considered yogurt.

If you are a fan of yogurt and use it regularly, you may want to repeat the preceding recipe using an 8-ounce reserved portion of the batch just made to start another. Continuing to do so will give you firsthand experience with the mutations (changes in flavor and texture) from one yogurt generation to the next, not to mention save you some money, too.

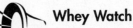

Whey Watch

Use whole milk for this recipe so you become familiar working with it. The yogurt-making process will also work with low-fat and nonfat milk, however.

Cheese Bite

You can improve the texture and nutrition of your yogurt by combining ¼ cup non-fat dry milk with 1 quart whole milk. Heat the mixture to 180°F and hold for 30 minutes. Quickly cool the milk to 115°F and add the yogurt.

Yogurt Cream Cheese

This recipe demonstrates the complete separation of whey from curd and provides firsthand experience of the proportions of liquids to solids in milk. The use of yogurt produces a fine cream cheese substitute with a slightly tangy flavor.

Yield: *1 cup*	
Prep time: 8 hours	

Ingredients:

1 qt. yogurt from Cultured Yogurt recipe

Equipment:

Stainless steel or plastic colander

Freshly laundered plain linen towel

1. Place the colander in a very clean sink or large vessel. Line the colander with the linen towel and carefully pour the yogurt into the towel. Fold the towel ends over to cover the yogurt and protect it. Allow the yogurt to drain at room temperature for 12 hours. If you prefer less tartness in your cream cheese, allow it to drain in the refrigerator.

2. Once the draining is complete, you may be surprised at the amount of whey collected. By volume, you should have about one cup more whey than cheese. Remember, as you read in the section on milk, the whey contains a fair amount of nutrition and includes most of the lactose. Do not be afraid to taste it. You will find it slightly tart, like a mild lemon water solution.

3. Move the yogurt cream cheese from the towel to a serving dish for immediate use, or to an airtight container and keep it refrigerated. Use the yogurt cream cheese as you would *crème fraîche* or mascarpone. It should be used within 1 week.

def•i•ni•tion

Crème fraîche, meaning "fresh cream," is the European version of sour cream. It is thicker and less tart than American sour cream and can be used in cooking without curdling. (Read more on crème fraîche in Chapter 6.)

Yogurt Dessert Cheese

This dip or topping for fruit uses the tartness of the yogurt to accent the sweetness of the honey. Together they create the perfect palette on which to place the spices.

Yield: *1 cup*
Prep time: 10 minutes

Ingredients:

1 cup yogurt cream cheese

2 tsp. honey

¼ tsp. cinnamon

¼ tsp. vanilla extract

¼ tsp. nutmeg

¼ tsp. allspice

Combine ingredients and serve with fruit such as fresh-cut apples.

Tasty Chatter
Yogurt Dessert Cheese is a wonderful complement to both sweet and tart fresh fruit. Serve over berries or use as a dip with dried tree fruits.

Cheese-Making Coagulants

In cheese making, enzymes are responsible for the formation of curd and flavor development. These enzymes can be proteolytic (break down protein) or lipolytic (break down fat).

Rennet contains a proteolytic enzyme responsible for breaking down casein and forming curd. A portion of the enzyme stays with the curd and continues to break down the amino acids during the aging process, producing desirable aromas and flavors.

The active ingredient in rennet is the enzyme chymosin, also called rennin. Its function in cheese making is to act on the milk protein casein and break the molecular bond which allows the protein to stay attached to water molecules. In the terminology of chemistry, this process is referred to as cleavage.

The word rennet has come to generically represent a whole host of dairy coagulants. Fortunately there are many sources of coagulating enzymes available. They fall into four classifications: animal, vegetable or plant extracts, microbial, and genetically engineered. Each has its advantages and shortcomings.

The starter bacteria used in cheese making also exhibit proteolytic activity along with what naturally occurs in the milk. This all comes into play during the aging process.

Animal Rennet

To the cheesemaker, a coagulant is an enzyme which acts on milk protein and causes the nearly complete separation of milk solids from the liquid. This step is called renneting. The term renneting comes from the word rennin, which represents the original complex of enzymes extracted from the inner mucosa of the fourth stomach chamber of young calves. Other animal-based rennet is also produced for specific types of milk. Traditionally, these options are kid goat rennet and lamb rennet for use in making goat and sheep milk cheeses, respectively.

> **Tasty Chatter**
>
> Long before the popularity of the vegan diet or the movement for more humane treatment of animals—predating the Roman Empire, in fact—a substitute for traditional rennet was much sought after. The production of animal rennet meant reducing one's herd of livestock. A calf turned to cow was far more valuable than a calf turned to rennet.

All mammal infants have the ability to produce the rennin enzyme critical to digestion and absorption of nutrition from their mother's milk. This includes human infants. If you want proof, feed a baby a bottle of warm milk, gently rock the child, then return the baby to its mother. You know what is going to happen. You will see the curds and whey from across the room. Yes, babies are cheesemakers, too.

Vegetable Rennet

The term *vegetable rennet* is often applied to both vegetable and microbial enzymes. This is a true representation in the sense that microbial coagulants are composed of single and multicellular microorganisums. The blending of the two terms also comes from the fact that both are considered appropriate for the vegan diet.

In both cases, the use of pure vegetable source rennet often adds a distasteful bitterness to aged cheeses. The bitterness can also be perceived in fresh-ripened cheeses. For this reason alone, pure vegetable rennet is not readily or commercially available. A product advertised as pure vegetable rennet is usually microbial and composed of mold spores.

GMO Rennet

Genetically modified (GMO) rennet is produced from microbial material (primarily fungi), in combination with calf genes and pepsin. The use of DNA material from the calf and the refinement of the resulting product has overcome the bitterness problem posed by pure vegetable rennet. It also eliminates the harvesting of animals to produce high-quality cheese. These coagulating agents, generically called GMO rennet, are used to produce the majority of the world's cheeses accounting for over 90 percent of the rennet used worldwide.

 Cheese Bite _____

Vegetable rennet taken from thistle is used in the Extremadura region of Spain to produce La Serena sheep's milk cheese.

What Matters Most About Rennet

Rennet is available in both liquid and dry form. The dry form can be either powder or tablet. Most will be in a concentrated form and can be rated from single to triple strength. This can be problematic for the hobby cheesemaker in that rennet is almost always perishable. Rennet does not really spoil in the sense that it becomes rotten. Its potency is diminished over time, and the rate of decline is greatly influenced by its environment. Liquid rennet has a maximum shelf life of three months, even when shipped and stored under perfect conditions. Liquid rennet must be kept refrigerated but cannot be frozen. Freezing will cause the formation of microscopic ice crystals, puncturing cell walls and destroying the enzymes.

Microbial rennet in tablet form is most convenient for the hobby cheesemaker, unless small batch sizes are desired. It is stable when frozen with a shelf life measured in years, and tablets are packaged individually to maintain product integrity. The tablets are scored, making them easy to break apart into the proper dose.

The recipes in this book all call for microbial rennet tablets. Going forward in this book, the word _rennet_ will be used generically to identify the cheese-making coagulants described so far and will specifically refer to the Marschall Microbial Coagulant brand for cheese making.

The Importance of Salt in Making Cheese

The role of salt in cheese making is threefold. Salt will obviously contribute to or enhance the flavor of cheese, as it does all foods. More importantly, salt is used to create and maintain an environment in which the desired bacterial agents will thrive and one which unwanted contaminants will find inhospitable. In this respect, salt may be considered a preservative. Salt also plays a role in controlling the actions of enzymes as they continue interacting with the cheese during aging.

Salt used in the cheese-making process must be of premium quality with absolutely no additives. The most common form is called flaked pickling salt or cheese salt. This is an extra fine grade salt that can be quickly and completely absorbed by cheese curds, providing even distribution while leaving no grit. As the name "pickling" implies, this salt is preferred for making the brines used in cheese making. All other salts are considered condiments with regard to cheese making and may have a place in finishing specialty cheeses.

A question you may have is "Can I make salt-free cheese?" The answer is yes, you can make some styles of cheese without additional salt. However, there is no way for the home cheesemaker to remove the natural sodium content of the milk. Whole milk contains 1½ grams of sodium per gallon, a portion of which is concentrated into the finished cheese.

All of the recipes in this book call for flaked pickling salt unless another type is specifically referenced. You will notice that the recipes, being designed for the home kitchen, are all given in volumetric units: quarts, gallons, teaspoons, tablespoons, and so on. In the industrial world, all recipes are considered formulas and use the common measurement of weight. This is critically important when it comes to the use of salt in a cheese recipe. Why? The fine, uniform grains of flaked salt that make it so perfect for cheese making also allow more salt to fit in less space. Coarser salts, such as kosher, have irregular shapes and allow for large gaps of air. This means that by volume, equal measures of each kind of salt will differ greatly in weight. On average, kosher salt will weigh almost a third less than flaked salt. For this reason, no salt substitutions should be made.

The Least You Need to Know

◆ How milk is processed determines its usability for cheese making.

◆ Milks from different species are not necessarily interchangeable.

◆ The four components of cheese are milk, starter cultures, coagulants, and salt.

◆ Cheese starters are bacterial cultures which consume milk sugar (lactose) and produce lactic acid.

◆ Coagulants, called rennet, are enzymes which break the molecular bond that connects milk solids to water, causing solid curds to be formed.

Chapter **3**

The Cheesemaker's Toolbox

In This Chapter

- ◆ Turning your kitchen into a creamery
- ◆ The everyday kitchen utensils needed to make cheese
- ◆ Simple but specialized cheese-making tools
- ◆ Unique equipment used by cheesemakers

In this chapter, you will find the list of required equipment for cheese making, most of which you probably already own. Each item is discussed in detail with attention paid to functionality and design. There are also items not considered to be standard kitchen wares. These are explained, along with their degree of necessity for the hobby cheesemaker.

Sizing Up Your Kitchen Creamery

Transitioning your kitchen into a cheese-making workshop will not require major renovations or remodeling. The cheese kitchen at Hale Farm and Historic Village outside Peninsula, Ohio, used to demonstrate cheese making as it was done on dairy farms in the 1860s, is little more than a 12×12-foot room lit by a single window. The room is equipped with a very small wood-burning stove, two sturdy work benches, and two walls of shelves—one set of shelves for equipment and another for drying cheeses. That's it.

The cheese kitchen at Hale Farm and Historic Village.

The recipes in this book have taken into account the cheese-making capacity of the average household kitchen. If you use your kitchen regularly, there is a very good chance you already own most of the basic equipment needed to make fresh and soft-ripened cheeses. There are a few necessary items which are not standard kitchen stock, but most of these are readily available at department stores or specialty kitchen shops. You can also find most of what you need at a local restaurant supply store.

The progression of cheese recipes in this book are arranged so that you are not required to purchase any specialized equipment until you are ready to move to the next level. It is important to note that when it comes to the unique devices required to make and age certain cheeses, you should not be tempted to become overly inventive. Attempting to devise homegrown equipment for cheese making is like building a rounder wheel. Over centuries of cheese making, the best tools and designs have managed to survive for one reason—they work.

Small-scale cheese making means a batch size starting with 1 to 4 gallons of milk. I have found that this range is easily managed in any home kitchen and that smaller batches may not provide enough curd for everything to work properly. This includes the aging of some cheeses. Keep this in mind as you take inventory of the equipment you already have. If you can handle 4 gallons of milk at the start of a recipe, you will be able to manage all of the recipes in this book.

Whey Watch

All vessels and utensils that come in contact with milk or curds must be made of stainless steel, enamel-lined steel, high-quality food-grade plastic, or glass. Since cheese making involves the acidification of milk (see Chapter 2), the use of aluminum or cast-iron utensils is not appropriate. Also, never use wooden spoons.

Must-Have Kitchen Basics

Ask any good butcher, baker, or chef what is most important to the quality of their work and they will tell you two things: the quality of the raw materials and the quality of their tools. Poorly designed or undersized kitchen wares can ruin the best of ingredients, regardless of your skill level.

For cheese making, this does not mean you have to go out and spend a fortune on name-brand, top-of-the-line, celebrity-endorsed, or restaurant-grade equipment. If you find that you need to purchase new or replace existing equipment, select function over appearance. Keep your eyes on the task you need the device to perform and the environment it must perform in.

The kitchen basics needed to make cheese.

Thermometer

The most important kitchen tool for cheese making is a high-quality thermometer with an accurate temperature range of at least 32°F to 212°F. When selecting a thermometer, accuracy and readability are the most important traits to look for. You must be able to trust that your thermometer will not lie to you, and you must be able to clearly note changes as small as 1°F.

Another essential feature of the thermometer is the ability to attach it securely to a vessel, so that your hands are free and you can continuously monitor its readings. There are many thermometers on the market that fit these criteria.

Avoid so-called "floating thermometers" designed to float upright in liquids. These contain very accurate mercury or alcohol thermometers that have a weighted end and are encased in glass tubes. Accuracy aside, they are slow to respond, difficult to read, and easy to break. They are only useful in cheese making while the cheese remains liquid (in milk form). For the same reason of fragility, precision glass laboratory thermometers are unsuitable as well.

Be sure not to confuse culinary thermometers with candy thermometers. Candy making and deep frying require temperatures well above the cheese-making range. This means that the visible resolution at lower temperatures will not be accurate. Analog dial thermometers can be used, provided the dial face is large enough to be read quickly and accurately and the response time is quick.

A digital culinary thermometer with a minimum 4-inch-long stainless steel probe is recommended. You will find the response time to be very quick with these instruments. Most digital culinary thermometers can accurately read from below freezing to over 400°F, making them perfect for all kitchen and food safety tasks.

The Cheese Pot

The terms cheese pot, stock pot, and kettle are used interchangeably by home cheesemakers. These terms all refer to a stainless steel (preferred) or enamel-lined pot with a capacity of at least 16 quarts for recipes using 3 gallons of milk. A 20-quart stock pot is ideal and will be required when making a 4-gallon batch of cheese. Your pot will need a fitted lid but it is not necessary for it to seal tightly.

The best kitchenware for cooking may not be the best for cheese making. Stock pots with heavy-clad bottoms are designed to diffuse heat evenly and avoid burning. These are excellent for cooking, but the additional mass in the bottom also retains heat for a longer period of time. This increases the time it will take for milk or curds to heat and, more importantly, to cool. If you have this type of cookware, you can use it, but you should experiment to determine how quickly it heats and cools. You can then adjust your procedures as needed. All of the procedures in this book assume that you are using basic kitchen kettles made of stainless or enameled steel with single-layer bottoms.

Some cheese styles will require you to have precise control over temperature changes and maintain a fixed temperature for extended periods of time. This is best accomplished with the use of a water bath or *bain-marie*. To create the bath apparatus, you will place the smaller cheese pot into a larger kettle. The larger kettle is then filled with water so that the water line and the milk line are close to even. It is important that the cheese pot not touch the bottom of the water kettle. The water forms a jacket around the cheese pot, and by controlling the temperature of the water you easily control the heat transfer to the milk.

Weights and Measures

A set of simple and functional measuring spoons are invaluable in any kitchen. Avoid gimmicky, adjustable-volume, one-size-fits-all devices. They are very useful for everyday cooking but not for cheese making. For cheese making, the plain, old-fashioned stainless steel or plastic sets with individual units (tablespoon, teaspoon, half teaspoon, and quarter teaspoon) will suffice. The construction materials used to fabricate these devices are pretty much the same. Look for moderately priced units rather than inexpensive ones. High-priced sets may be more durable, but the precision should be the same as moderately priced sets.

The recipes in this book all use commercial creamery starter cultures. These cultures are provided in bulk form and are intended for large volumes of milk. It will therefore be necessary to measure out amounts smaller than the standard quarter teaspoon. This is the smidgen, pinch, and

Whey Watch

Cheaply made and therefore inexpensive measuring devices will most likely have sacrificed accuracy for price.

dash factor grandma talks about, except not quite that elementary. I refer to these units of measure as ⅛, ¹⁄₁₆, and ¹⁄₃₂ teaspoon. And yes, you can purchase sets of measuring spoons that include these units.

At some point, you will encounter recipes expressed in weight not volume. In cheese making, milk is often referenced in pounds or kilograms. Other recipes may use liters as a measure of volume. A gallon of whole milk weighs 8.6 pounds, has a specific gravity of 1.032, and contains 3.8 liters (or 4 quarts or 8 pints or 16 cups).

In the United States, the gallon is the standard retail unit of measure for milk. For that reason, home cheese making is just easier if milk is used by the gallon, quart, pint, or cup. You can purchase smaller volumes when a recipe calls for less than a gallon, but working in gallons will be more economical. If you are using your own animal's milk or dividing up a gallon of store-bought milk, an accurate, 1-quart glass measuring cup is perfect. To get the most for your money, select one that can be heated and used in a microwave.

The timing of events during the cheese-making process is as critical to success as the quality of the ingredients. Paying close attention to a good-quality kitchen timer will ensure that you stay on pace. Distractions are inevitable, and nothing is more disappointing than missing a critical step over the lack of a buzzer. Your timer need only measure minutes and be reliable. A digital timer is your best bet, provided it is in a convenient location—even your oven's timer will do. Portable spring-wound models that are checked for accuracy as they age may be preferred over digital battery-operated timers since there is a risk that the battery will give out during use.

Kitchen Utensils

In taking inventory of your kitchen utensils, measure everything against your cheese pot. You must be able to reach the bottom of the kettle without getting your hand into it. If you can avoid getting wet while placing the utensil crosswise in the kettle (bottom left to upper right), all the better. Anything else is going to be too small. Do not use wooden spoons, and whenever possible avoid utensils with wooden handles unless you can totally prevent the wood from coming into contact with the milk or curd. Wooden cooking utensils may harbor harmful or unwanted bacteria that can only be destroyed by washing in harsh chemicals or treating with high heat, both of which may damage the tool. This makes wood a bad investment. A few extra dollars spent in this area will pay you back many times over. Remember to shop for the right size, not the super size.

A slotted mixing spoon will get the most use in cheese making. I prefer a slotted spoon over a solid one because it blends ingredients more quickly and evenly. In cheese making, overstirring can be a problem. The slots also allow whey to drain away from the curds as they are transferred from one vessel to another.

A perforated skimming ladle with a wide, shallow bowl is needed to carefully remove curds from whey or hot water. The diameter of the bowl should be as large as possible while still allowing the ladle to slip down the side of the cheese pot and scoop under the curd.

Cheese Bite

Milk has been used as the base liquid in paint for centuries due to the bonding properties of casein protein. When hot milk is allowed to cool on a surface, it will stick and stick hard. Utensils should be rinsed clean with *cold* water after each time they make contact with milk and before washing with hot, soapy water.

A colander with a capacity of 6 to 8 quarts will be needed to hold draining curds. Once again, use the cheese pot as your guide. The strainer should sit securely on the rim and allow whey to drain into the kettle.

Know Your Stove

Not all stove tops are alike. The temperature settings indicated on the controls are relative only to the stove itself. "Medium" is not a thermometer reading. It is an indication of temperature about midway between low and high for the specific burner it controls. If your stove or oven has specific thermometer settings, you should confirm their accuracy. Do this by heating water and matching the actual temperature with the preset indicator.

The greatest difference in heat sources is between gas and electric. Gas stoves are instant on and instant off, with minimal heat retention in the burner grate. The transfer of heat to a cooking vessel is best described as gentle. Gas has the added benefit of near-infinite adjustment. Electric burners are slow to heat up and very slow to cool. A cooking vessel placed in direct contact with the burner may cause hot spots and promote scorching. If you have a conventional electric stove top, you will find that using the water bath (bain-marie) heating method described previously works best. You may also consider using a burner trivet to hold the cooking vessel slightly above the burner.

Whey Watch _____

If you are using an electric stove top, remember that when a recipe tells you to turn off the heat, you must remove the kettle from the hot burner.

If you have a flat-top stove, review the manufacturer's recommendations for using the stove with large stockpots. There may be restrictions on the surface area that can be covered and/or the amount of weight the stove can support. Make sure that your cheese making does not wind up voiding your warranty.

The stove settings and times given throughout this book are based on a standard home-use natural gas stove top with average heat output.

Special Cheese-Making Equipment

The specialized equipment used by home cheesemakers is not complicated or even all that specialized. You may find these items locally and they are certainly available on the Internet. The same attention to functionality applies here as it does to basic kitchen equipment.

Specialized cheese-making equipment.

Curd Knife

You will need to be able to cut curds into uniform smaller pieces. The sizes of the pieces are specific to the type of cheese you are making. The curd at this point will be much like Jell-O, so a sharp edge is not required. Your curd knife must be long enough to reach the bottom of the cheese pot without the handle touching the cheese.

A long-bladed carving or bread knife can be used. A better choice is a 12-inch stainless steel icing spatula.

Cheesecloth

You will need cheesecloth, a word that can mean different things to different people. Cheesecloth is made of 100 percent cotton threads that are bleached to give it a clean white appearance. The unbleached version is called muslin. Like most woven fabrics, cheesecloth is graded by thread count. There are many grades of cheesecloth with many uses. Cheesemakers primarily use two grades, commonly called coarse and fine. Coarse cheesecloth is rated as #10 with about 20 threads per square inch. Fine cheesecloth is rated as #60 with a thread count of around 30. Expect slight variations between manufacturers. Coarse cheesecloth is used when pressing hard cheese into a solid curd mass and is best for use as a cover during air drying. Fine cloth will be needed for thin curd and softer cheeses. Have enough of each to allow you to increase the thread count by using double or triple layers as needed.

Cheese Bite

Some cheese-making recipes may reference "butter muslin." This is a very fine weave (90 threads per inch) of unbleached cotton thread. You can substitute for this with three or four layers of fine cheesecloth.

In the next chapter, you'll learn how to prepare and use cheesecloth.

Drying Mats

Drying mats are simple platforms that hold resting cheeses as they dry and/or ripen. Their important features are the grooves or gaps on the surface that allow air to keep the bottom of the cheese dry. Kitchen cooling racks with wide gaps between thin metal wires are not suitable for this, because the weight of the cheese may cause the wires to cut into the bottom surface. The hobbyist will find that bamboo sushi rolling mats work perfectly well.

Cheese Boards

Cheese boards are a set of paddlelike tools with grooved surfaces used to turn cheeses that are shaped using hoops or open-ended molds (more on this in a minute). Their size is dependent on the application. The boards are placed on either end (top and bottom) of a curd-filled mold, creating a draining mold sandwich. The whole assembly is periodically flipped over to facilitate draining and shaping. The hobby cheesemaker will find that any two food-grade flat surfaces of the right size can be used. Anything from saucers to trivets will work.

Cheese Wax

The maturing (aging) of some cheeses requires that small amounts of gases, including oxygen, be allowed to pass through the protective wrapping. This is traditionally done by sealing the cheese with a special grade of wax. Other cheese must be stored under *anaerobic* conditions—this means preventing the cheese from coming into contact with the surrounding air. To accomplish this, the surface is completely and securely wrapped in a protective seal, which is best done by vacuum packing.

def•i•ni•tion

Anaerobic describes the metabolism of a living organism that thrives in the absence of oxygen. This is a key element to cheese making because many of the unwanted or harmful bacteria require oxygen.

Cheese wax is designed with the special qualities needed by cheesemakers. It melts at relatively low temperature so it will not "cook" the cheese as it is applied. Melted wax is easily applied to the cheese by dipping. Bubbles or gaps on the surface of a waxed cheese can be painted over with a small food-grade brush. The thin layers of hot wax on the cheese sets (hardens) quickly (seconds not minutes) at room temperature. The wax remains pliable at moderately cool temperatures, allowing the cheese a fair amount of flexibility to expand and contract without breaking the seal. Finally, cheese wax is as easy to cut through as the cheese itself.

An alternative to wax is a high-quality food storage vacuum system to seal your cheese for aging. You can get excellent results with this method and will appreciate the ease with which you can sample aging cheeses and then reseal them. If you have a vacuum sealer and are not comfortable with the traditional waxing method, try it. You must use the air-proof packaging recommended by the system's manufacturer. However, it's not necessary to invest in a vacuum packaging system solely for cheese making. Waxing is far more economical.

Draining and Shaping Molds

The devices used to shape cheese are called molds or hoops. Many cheeses can be recognized by their shape and size alone. Often the shape of the cheese comes from regional traditions and/or different interpretations of the same cheese. *Gouda* is a perfect example with its distinctive rounded edge and slightly bulging top and bottom. The small but identically shaped versions are recognized worldwide as Baby Gouda. The flavor and texture of Gouda is not dependent on the physical characteristics and can be produced in many shapes and sizes without a noticeable loss of character.

Shape and size can be very important to successful development of the desired characteristics in cheese, with size being the more influential of the two. In those instances where shape and size contribute to overall development, specific molds are employed to form the shape, determine density, control moisture content, define the surface area and texture, and determine the size.

def•i•ni•tion

Gouda is an aged hard cheese made from cow's milk and is named after the city of Gouda, in the Netherlands. The name Gouda is not protected by trademark or copyright, meaning that you cannot assume the cheese you purchase is actually produced in its namesake town. Look for "Product of the Netherlands" on the label for the real thing.

Camembert, for instance, is always the same diameter, thickness, and weight—all of which control the ripening time, growth of surface mold, flavor, and internal texture. Brie, regardless of diameter, will always be the same thickness as Camembert. Both cheeses are made in similar ways and share the same flavor and texture due to the common thickness.

Advanced Cheese-Making Equipment

A few pieces of highly specialized equipment used in commercial cheese operations need to be explained. Nothing that follows is absolutely required to make your own cheese; however, you may want to have an original or at least a reasonable and functional facsimile. Where possible, I have provided alternative methods and suggested substitutes.

Cheese Press

No piece of cheese-making equipment is more misunderstood than the cheese press. The name implies a purpose rather than a process. When you hear "cheese press," you may envision a machine resembling a wine press, leading to thoughts of using brute force to wring the whey out of cheese curds. But it is just not like that. Pressing cheese is more about squeezing than about compressing or extracting liquid. The application of pressure to fresh curds is called "pressing," and the process will cause some liquid to be pushed out from between pieces of curd. This is good; however, it is not the sole reason for pressing. For the cheese press to work, most of the free whey must already be drained off the curds.

When curds are squeezed, their surfaces are stretched and the very thin layer of fat that surrounds them is split open. This exposes the milk protein matrix within. Remember that those protein molecules, under the influence of lactic acid and rennet enzyme, are in attraction mode. When exposed to one another they will bond, known as knitting to the cheesemaker. This is the process where loose cheese curds become solid cheese. To the novice, it may appear that the curds are simply "pressed" or mechanically packed together, but the atomic bond between molecules is far stronger than any created by pressure alone.

There are many devices out there which profess to be cheese presses. It appears that the more sophisticated they look, the worse they perform. No other piece of cheese-making equipment inspires more inventiveness or tinkering. Contraptions with spring-loaded pressure bars, fixed levers with dangling weights, screw-driven pressure plates—it seems everyone has their own idea of what a cheese press should be. Remember that simple is best.

Whey Watch

A cheese press is only required if you intend to make hard cheese. In all other recipes requiring some time under pressure, you will find instructions for using everyday items to do the job.

Your cheese press must have certain design features, the most important being that it is the correct capacity. Capacity means the ability to hold the necessary volume of curd needed to produce the desired diameter and height of the finished cheese. The press must evenly support 50 pounds of weight. Liquid must be allowed to easily drain away from the curd and press.

All you will need for home cheese making is a 7×4-inch classic Tomme cheese basket with a matching follower. The Tomme (pronounced tum) is a basket-style mold with small holes in the sides and bottom to allow the draining of excess whey. The follower (sometimes referred to as a top or lid) fits inside the basket with just enough clearance to prevent binding against the sides and has a flat surface on one side with a support structure on the other. The supports distribute weight evenly over the surface on the flat side. The Tomme press forms cheese into the classic wheel shape.

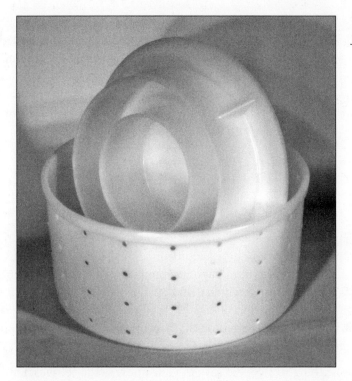

Tomme cheese basket with follower.

A visit to your local used sporting goods store or flea market will net you the perfect set of operating weights for the Tomme press. All you will need are a few old style barbell weight disks. Look for ones that have flat surfaces and clear heaviness markings. Table 3.1 shows the total range of weights you need for home cheese making. Just be sure that the diameter of the heaviest is less than that of the follower.

Table 3.1: Barbell Weights for Pressing Cheese

Quantity	Weight	Total
2	2 pounds	4 pounds
2	3 pounds	6 pounds
2	5 pounds	10 pounds
3	10 pounds	30 pounds
	Total	50 pounds

Cheese Bite _____

If barbell weights are not an option, you can use water. A 1-gallon plastic milk jug full of water weighs approximately 8 pounds. Simple math will give you any weight factor you need up to that amount.

The simple design of the Tomme press, with only two working parts plus inexpensive barbell weights, is easy to use and cleans up in a snap. A Tomme-style press is regularly used in commercial creameries. This pressing system has the capacity to press curd from 3 to 4 gallons of milk with constant pressure and without the need for regular adjustments. Specific instruction for using a cheese press will be given in Chapter 9.

Cheese Cave

Proper ripening and aging of some cheese styles requires that the cheese be stored in an environment conducive to promoting development of the desired characteristics, such as white bloom mold, while discouraging unwanted elements like black mold. This means controlling temperature, humidity, and air flow. This is done with what is called a cheese cave. Precise control is outside the abilities of the average cheese-making hobbyist, but there are simple methods and devices that will let you control what you can and monitor how you are doing.

Probably the closest thing to a cheese cave in your house is the refrigerator. It holds a pretty consistent cool temperature, stays relatively clean, and receives occasional fresh air. Humidity can be an issue, however. The colder an environment is, the less moisture the air is capable of retaining.

Most mold-ripened cheeses will need the humidity to be much higher than your refrigerator will allow. You can compensate for this by placing your cheese in a large plastic storage container with a fitted lid. Placing one or more containers of water alongside the cheese will also provide moisture. The humidity can then be controlled by adjusting the fit of the container's lid. The downside of using your refrigerator as a cheese cave is that the temperature will be too low for most cheeses and the cheese may take up considerable space.

Dedicating a small refrigerator to cheese making will solve the space problem. Look for a device that is UL approved and rated for 110 volts—this can be identified by the standard three-prong plug. The temperature can be controlled with an external thermostat. This is an industrial-grade device designed to override the internal thermostat of the refrigerator. The control box sits outside and has a probe that monitors the temperature inside. The temperature can be set and adjusted until the desired point is reached. The humidity in a dedicated refrigerator can be increased by maintaining an open container of water on the bottom shelf. Different humidity levels for different cheese styles can be managed using the plastic container described previously.

Small refrigerator dedicated to cheese.

If you are going to the expense of setting up a cheese cave, the best investment you can make is a wireless weather monitor. This gadget is placed outside and sends environment data to a receiver inside. The less costly versions that monitor only temperature and humidity are perfect for a cheese cave. Regardless of where in the house you place your cheese cave, you will know what is happening. Less expensive hard-wired versions are also available.

Cheese Trier

The cheese trier is a classic piece of cheese-making equipment. A professional-grade cheese trier is expensive (in excess of $100), and is not practical for the hobbyist because homemade cheese wheels will be much smaller than those of a commercial creamery.

The device allows the cheesemaker to extract a core sample of an aging cheese and inspect the interior. The cheese can be examined for texture, aroma, flavor, and the progress of interior mold development. The trier is inserted into the cheese and, when twisted, cuts the core, which is then pulled out. After examination, the core is reinserted, filling the hole and leaving the cheese intact to continue aging. Other than actually cutting a small cheese open, there is no other option for the small-scale cheesemaker.

pH Meter

Here is the quick and simple explanation of pH. The pH scale is used to determine acidity or alkalinity (lack of acidity) relative to water. Pure water at 77°F is said to have a pH of 7 (meaning neutral). This is an established standard recognized worldwide. A pH of less than 7 is considered acidic (the smaller the number, the stronger the acid). A number greater than 7 indicates alkalinity. The pH of fresh milk is 6.7. You have already learned the importance of lactic and other acids in cheese making, and a pH meter is the tool used to monitor the progress of acid development.

There are tools other than the pH meter that can be used to monitor progress, but the *degree of resolution* needed to be useful can be difficult to discern. Yes, the advanced hobbyist will want a pH meter, however, any home cheesemaker closely following the recipes in this book will do fine without one.

def•i•ni•tion

Degree of resolution is the distance between two of the smallest reference points on a calibrated scale. A 12-inch ruler marked into 48 equal segments has a resolution of ¼ inch.

You do not need to rush out and purchase all of the items presented in the chapter. Each will be reintroduced in the chapters where it is used. Detailed instructions on using the special-purpose items are given within each recipe where they are used. There may be other tools and gadgets you know of that would be well suited to one or more cheese-making tasks. Work with what is listed here, and if you find an item troublesome, then look for an alternative. Doing so will help you spend your money wisely.

Preparing for a Cheese-Making Session

The small-scale cheesemaker will find that a neat, clean kitchen of any size provides ample space to work comfortably. It is very important that you dedicate your kitchen to making cheese until the end of the session. You should not prepare any other food products while you are preparing cheese. You will be working with warm milk and must be aware that the milk is very susceptible to unwanted bacterial infection. It is not difficult to prevent sanitation and cross-contamination problems as long as you use due care.

To prepare your work area, first put all food products away; remove all dish cloths and soiled towels to the laundry room; and wash your counters, sink, and stove top with an appropriate cleanser. Next use a commercial antibacterial or disinfectant cleaning spray to wipe down all surfaces. A solution of 1 teaspoon of household bleach in 1 pint of cold water will also work, provided that your countertops do not react with chlorine. If you have any doubts, check the manufacturer's recommendation.

At the start of a session, determine and collect all the equipment that will be used. Everything should be washed and sanitized prior to each cheese-making session. In a commercial creamery, sanitation is taken almost as seriously as it is in a hospital operating room. Many of the same cleansers and sanitizing chemicals are used. Iodophor, a concentrated combination of iodine and detergent, is used extensively in the dairy industry. However, it is not practical for use in a household kitchen because of the brownish-red stains it leaves on everything except stainless steel and glass. There are other chemical sanitizers available.

Whey Watch

Do not leave milk out of the refrigerator for an extended length of time. Milk should be kept refrigerated until it is called for in the process.

Household bleach has been recommended as a sanitizing agent for many years, but it should never be used on stainless steel. The chlorine will react with the stainless alloy and cause it to deteriorate. Reserve the use of bleach for sanitizing the work area as described previously. A product called Easy-Clean Cleanser, available at beer- and winemaking shops, is preferred. The chemical uses oxygen to disinfect all surface materials without the need for rinsing. It is economical, safe, and efficient. If you prefer not to use chemical agents, you will need to process your equipment in boiling water. Boiling water is also the best way to sterilize cheesecloth.

Place your prepared equipment within easy reach of your work area, and you're ready to get started.

The Least You Need to Know

◆ Only use materials suited to working with acidic foods, such as stainless steel.

◆ Temperature accuracy and control are very important, including that of your stove burners and refrigerator.

◆ Make sure the size of your equipment (bowls, refrigerator space) fits the task.

♦ It is better to purchase the right equipment and utensils than to try and reinvent them.

♦ Proper preparation for a cheese-making session includes a clean and sanitary work space and access to all equipment and utensils within arm's reach.

Part 2

Making Quick Cheeses

At this point, you have enough information to be dangerous, so now we put that knowledge to work. You will start with a few simple cheese recipes designed to build your skills for handling milk and other dairy products. Best of all, these cheeses are ready to eat as soon as they are done. Many of the projects include a traditional recipe using your completed cheese as the primary ingredient.

4

Cheese by Direct Acidification

In This Chapter

- Using acids to make cheese
- Working with cheesecloth
- Three types of fresh cheese

The next time someone points a camera at you and says, "Say cheese!" instead of just grinning from ear to ear, you can now think, "Cheese? I know cheese." Taking all you've learned to this point, in this chapter we are going to start making cheese. But first there are just a few more things you need to know.

Making Direct-Acid Cheeses

In Chapter 3, you learned all about the usage and importance of bacterial agents and their role in creating acidity in milk. There is yet another way to do this, called direct acidification. In this method, an acid is added directly to the milk rather than using the slower process of fermentation. You may be thinking that adding acid rather than naturally producing it sounds like cheating. Rest assured, it is not a modern invention for making instant cheese. The use of acids is documented as one of the oldest known cheese-making methods. In many premodern cultures, making this type of cheese was a daily task. After the morning milking, the cheese would be prepared and served with that evening's meal. Table 4.1 lists a few common acids and the cheese they produce.

Table 4.1: Common Acids Used to Produce Direct-Acid Cheeses

Acid	Cheese	Milk	Cuisine
Vinegar	Queso Blanco	Cow	Spanish
Lemon Juice	Paneer	Cow	Indian
Lemon Juice	Beyaz Peynir	Sheep	Turkish
Tartaric	Mascarpone	Cow	American

All cheeses made by the direct addition of acids are considered to be in the fresh cheese category. This is because there will be no bacterial agents present to conduct an aging or ripening process. The cheeses made using this method should be consumed as soon as they are ready.

Adding acid directly to heated milk causes the same reaction as bacterial acidification described in Chapter 2, but without the need for fermentation. The milk's response is almost immediate. The increase in acidity changes the polarity of the protein molecules. The molecules are then attracted to each other, forming the matrix described in Chapter 2. The microscopic net gathers the fat globules along with other milk solids, creating semi-solid curds. The milk will appear to have thickened.

How to Use Cheesecloth

A skill required by every cheesemaker is the ability to make a cheesecloth draining bag. So before we go any further, we'll show you how it's done.

First, for the cheesecloth, please do not be tempted to use an old pillowcase, man's handkerchief, pantyhose, tea towel, or any of the other things you may see suggested on the Internet. They may work, but you will not learn what you need to know.

If you have not already done so, find a local fabric store, or reference Appendix B for an online retailer, and purchase 2 yards of both coarse and fine cheesecloth as described in Chapter 3. (Remember, coarse cheesecloth is used for hard cheese, fine is for soft cheese.) Cut each in half, and keep one half as it is (1 square yard). The other can be resized as needed later on.

Prior to each use, you must sanitize the cheesecloth by placing it in a saucepan filled with water. Bring the water to a boil and shut off heat. Place a colander over the sink drain and pour the water through it, catching the cloth. This will also sanitize the colander. Leave them both in the sink, as is, until they are called for.

Next, you can practice making the draining bag by using items in your kitchen, such as dry beans or rice, to act as the curds.

First, dampen your sanitized cheese-cloth and place it over a large bowl. Place a bag of dry beans or rice onto the cheese-cloth in the bowl. Lift three corners of the cloth as high as you can over the center of the mock curd mass without disturbing it. This will form three strands of cloth. Hold these three in one hand while the other hand lifts the fourth corner. Wrap the fourth strand around the first three at a point about halfway between the curds and the ends. Tuck strand four under itself and pull it snug. The bag is now closed.

Whey Watch _____

Cheesecloth shrinks after being processed in boiling water and allowed to dry. The minimum sizes given in recipes are based on preshrunk cheesecloth. To avoid coming up short, purchase a whole piece of cheesecloth 1 square yard or more, then cut it to size after the initial boiling once it is dry.

Steps to creating a cheesecloth draining bag.

To hang the bag, separate the ends of the first three strands into two groups (1 end and 2 ends). Tie these ends into a loose square knot. This will form a loop that can be hung over a sink faucet or cupboard knob.

Practice making the draining bag several times before making cheese to avoid endangering your real curds.

Paneer Indian Cheese

Indian paneer is a fresh cheese that has the versatile characteristics of tofu. The flavor is very bland, taking on the flavors
of whatever it is used in. The texture is firm, almost meatlike,
making it a good meat substitute.

Yield: *8 ounces*
Cook time: 30 minutes
Rest time: 1 hour

Ingredients:

½ gallon cow's milk (raw is fine)

¼ cup fresh-squeezed lemon juice

Equipment:

3 or 4 qt. saucepan

Spoon (not wooden)

Colander

Fine cheesecloth (at least 18 inches square)

1. Prepare the fine cheesecloth for use, as described previously.

2. Place milk in the saucepan and bring to a boil, stirring frequently to prevent scorching. Turn off heat. If you have
   an electric stove, remember to remove the pan from the
   burner.

> ### Tasty Chatter
>
> This paneer recipe uses only milk and lemon juice to produce
> a firm fresh cheese. The process used is rustic. It relies on your
> observations rather than precision instruments to determine when
> enough is enough. With this recipe, you're learning how to pre-
> pare and use cheesecloth and work with scalding hot milk.

3. Use a tablespoon to add lemon juice, 2 tablespoons at a
   time, while constantly stirring. As lemon juice is added, you
   will see curds start to form and the liquid will change from
   opaque white to semi-translucent, similar to skim milk.
   Continue adding lemon juice until curds completely separate and whey changes to translucent watery green. There
   is no rush. After separation, allow the saucepan of curds and
   whey to cool on the stove for about 30 minutes.

Whey Watch _____

Use a back-and-forth or up-and-down motion when stirring milk during cheese making. Do not stir the milk in a circular motion. Doing so generates a vortex and will cause heavier ingredients, including curd, to collect in the center rather than be evenly distributed.

4. Line the colander with cheesecloth and place under the sink faucet. Carefully pour curds and whey into the cheesecloth. Rinse and cool curds for 15 seconds, using a light sprinkle or spray of cold water.

5. Lift the corners of the cheesecloth, making it a draining bag of cheese curd. Hang the bag so whey can drain from curds. Allow the bag to hang until it stops dripping (about 15 minutes). The more water you remove, the drier the cheese will be.

6. Open the cheesecloth on a flat surface. Use your hands to form curds into a disk just under 2 inches thick. Size is important because the cheese is going to be squeezed into a thick pancake by a heavy weight. Fold the cheesecloth edges over the disk, distributing the cloth evenly around the cheese. Avoid heavy wrinkles.

7. Set the wrapped cheese on a flat, rimmed surface so that whey can be collected. A pie dish or rimmed baking sheet will do. Place a heavy frying pan on top of the cheese. Be careful to keep everything level. You can use canned goods to add additional weight. Cheese should be pressed for 30 minutes, then whey should be discarded and cheese turned over and pressed for another 30 minutes.

8. Remove cheese from the cheesecloth. This cheese is best used fresh. It may be stored in the refrigerator for up to 4 days by placing it in an airtight container with a small amount of water to keep it moist.

Cheese Bite _____

Rinse used cheese-cloth with cold water to remove any residue. Boil the washed cloth and hang to dry. Store the dry, clean cloth in a zip-lock bag.

Saag Paneer

Saag Paneer is a warm vegetarian dish featuring spinach and paneer prepared in a spicy curry sauce.

Yield: *4 1-cup servings*

Prep time: 20 minutes

Cook time: 30 minutes

Ingredients:

2 TB. vegetable oil

8 oz. paneer, cut into ¾-inch cubes

1 onion, diced

3 cloves garlic, minced

2 to 3 hot chile peppers, seeded and minced

1 TB. minced ginger

1 TB. curry powder

2 tsp. ground cumin

1 tsp. ground coriander

2 10-oz. pkg. frozen spinach, thawed and squeezed dry

1 cup plain yogurt

½ cup cilantro, chopped

> **Tasty Chatter**
>
> Paneer is used to prepare many traditional Indian dishes. This recipe for Saag Paneer demonstrates the use of the cheese to add body and increased nutrition to leafy greens. The cheese is handled in much the same way as you would tofu.

1. Heat 1 tablespoon oil in a nonstick pan over medium heat. It is important for the pan to be nonstick since paneer has a tendency to stick to other cookware.

2. Add cubes of paneer and cook until golden brown. Remove cheese from the pan and reserve.

3. Place remaining oil in the pan and sauté onion, garlic, chiles, and ginger until onions are translucent.

4. Add curry, cumin, and coriander and sauté until spices become fragrant.

5. Drain spinach and add to the pan. Continue to sauté until spinach is heated through. Then stir in yogurt until heated.

6. Return reserved paneer and stir in until it is reheated.

7. Serve over rice garnished with cilantro.

Queso Blanco

This fresh cheese originated in Spain and is now a popular dietary staple in South America.

Ingredients:

1 gallon milk (raw milk as well as goat milk are fine)

¼ cup vinegar (apple cider vinegar is traditionally used)

½ tsp. flaked salt

Equipment:

Measuring cups

Thermometer

Cheese pot

Mixing spoon

Colander

Fine cheesecloth

Yield: *1 to 1½ pounds*	
Cook time: 30 minutes	
Rest time: 1 hour	

Tasty Chatter

In this recipe, you will use precision measurements to make queso blanco. You will find the process to be very much like paneer, but the volume of the batch is doubled to yield more cheese and provide experience dealing with more milk. The use of a thermometer will help you understand how your stove top is responding to your needs.

1. Prepare the cheesecloth as previously described.

2. Place milk into the cheese pot over medium heat. Stir occasionally to keep milk from scorching and distribute heat evenly. Check the temperature periodically until milk reaches 195°F.

3. Add vinegar and stir to combine. Remove the pot from heat and let it set for 5 minutes. During this time, curds and whey will fully separate.

4. Carefully remove as much whey as you can without discarding curds. This is best done by placing the pot at the edge of a sink and tipping it slightly to pour off the liquid.

5. Add salt to drained curds and gently fold in.

6. Using a slotted spoon or small strainer, transfer curds to a cheesecloth-lined colander or strainer. Tie the corners to

make a draining bag and hang the ball of draining cheese over a sink or bowl for 1 hour. Cheese will form a solid mass as it drains.

7. Remove finished cheese from the cheesecloth and place in an airtight container or wrap in plastic food wrap. This cheese will keep refrigerated for 1 week.

Mascarpone

Mascarpone is called a double or triple cream cheese and is made from cow's milk. This cheese originated in the Lombardy region of Italy in the late sixteenth or early seventeenth century. It is ivory colored and ranges in texture from thickened cream to softened butter.

The direct acidifying agent used in this recipe is food-grade tartaric acid. This is a common winemaking additive and is available from homebrewing and winemaking supply shops. It must be in pure granular form.

Yield: *13 to 14 ounces*

Cook time: 20 minutes

Rest time: 10 to 12 hours

Ingredients:
¼ tsp. tartaric acid
1 TB. distilled water
1 qt. light or heavy cream

Equipment:
2 qt. or larger double boiler
Mixing spoon
Measuring spoons
Colander
1 yard fine cheesecloth (prepared for use)

1. Combine tartaric acid with distilled water in a small cup. Be sure acid is completely dissolved.

2. Place light cream in a double boiler or large bowl set over a smaller pot containing water. Make sure the bottom of the bowl does not touch the water. Bring the water in the pot to a boil and heat cream until it reaches 185°F. Stir occasionally to evenly distribute heat.

3. Turn off heat and carefully move the hot bowl of cream from the water pot to a protected countertop.

4. Stir in dissolved tartaric acid until a fine curd forms. This should be visible around the sides of your bowl. When using light cream, it will look like slightly curdled milk. This will be more pronounced if you are using half-and-half. Let cream cool for 5 to 10 minutes, stirring occasionally.

5. Line the colander with a double thickness of fine cheesecloth and set over a deep bowl. Pour cream mixture into strainer. You may have to do this gradually to allow some whey to drain before pouring more. When all has been poured into the strainer, gather the cheesecloth corners and tie a loose knot (or use a short piece of kitchen twine or a twist tie) to secure the cloth.

6. Lift the colander and discard whey. Put the colander back into the bowl and place the whole apparatus in the refrigerator for 10 hours or overnight.

7. Remove the cheese assembly from the refrigerator and discard bowl contents. Open the cheesecloth and extract mascarpone. The cheese should be kept refrigerated in an airtight container and consumed within 1 week.

> ### Tasty Chatter
> Mascarpone can be used in sweet and savory dishes, but is best known as an ingredient in tiramisu.

Cheesy Polenta Bake

Soft and mild on its own, polenta is topped nicely with mascarpone cheese, basil pesto, and *Parmigiano-Reggiano* to create a creamy, salty, and nutty herb appetizer or snack. Polenta is the Italian version of cornmeal mush or grits. It is a staple in northern Italy that works as a base for meats and sauces or is simply served with butter and Parmigiano-Reggiano cheese.

Ingredients:

1 TB. extra-virgin olive oil

1 16-oz. roll readymade polenta

½ cup mascarpone cheese

2 TB. prepared basil pesto

¾ cup finely grated Parmigiano-Reggiano cheese

> **Yield:** *8 3-oz. servings*
>
> **Prep time:** 10 minutes
>
> **Cook time:** 15 to 18 minutes

1. Coat the bottom of a 13×9 baking pan with olive oil. Slice polenta into ⅓-inch slices and layer snugly in pan.

2. Mix mascarpone with pesto and spread over top of polenta. Sprinkle with grated cheese.

3. Bake at 450°F for 15 to 18 minutes or until lightly browned and bubbly.

def•i•ni•tion

Parmigiano-Reggiano is always made using raw cow's milk. This cheese is produced exclusively in the Parma region of Italy. Cheese made in the same style anywhere else in the world is only called Parmesan.

The Cheesemaker's Apprentice

If you have successfully completed the cheese recipes in this chapter, you have earned the title of apprentice home cheesemaker. Many home cheesemakers are satisfied at this point and find great reward in preparing and using these simple and functional cheeses. The culinary possibilities are endless, and anyone who tries your cheese will be impressed that you made it yourself from scratch.

You now have the experience and should have the confidence to move forward. The title of apprentice implies that you are learning through practice and want to learn more. All that you have learned so far will be needed in the chapters ahead.

The Least You Need to Know

◆ Direct acidification is a method that adds acid directly to the milk and can yield a variety of fresh cheeses.

◆ The proper preparation and use of cheesecloth are critical steps in cheese making.

◆ Practice making paneer, queso blanco, and mascarpone cheeses before proceeding to other varieties to gain a hands-on understanding of how milk becomes cheese.

Chapter 5

Making Mozzarella

In This Chapter

- ♦ The use of rennet and calcium chloride in cheese
- ♦ How to make mozzarella cheese
- ♦ Troubleshooting a problem cheese
- ♦ Ricotta, the cheese made of cheese that is not a cheese

If there is one word that will instantly bring cheese to mind, that word is *pizza*, and pizza means mozzarella.

Traditional mozzarella is made using cultured acidification and requires extensive analysis of the cheese milk chemistry. The direct acidification method used in this chapter is quick, easy, and produces a great cheese. In this chapter, you will find a recipe for American-style mozzarella or "pizza cheese."

More Cheese-Making Ingredients

In the following version of mozzarella-style pizza cheese, you will get your first experience with some ingredients that are unique to cheese making. You will need some of the items that were introduced in Chapter 2: calcium chloride solution, rennet milk coagulant, and flaked salt. You will also need food-grade citric acid and distilled water.

Citric acid is a common food additive. It is what makes sour candy so sour and adjusts the pH of canned goods for safe storage. For cheese, do not use the inexpensive citric acid used to make bath salts. It must be at least food-grade quality, up to pharmaceutical grade. You will find the right variety in any good winemaking supply shop. You want it in dry, granular form. It should be stored in an airtight container in a cool, dry environment.

def•i•ni•tion

Distillation is a purification process whereby a liquid such as water is transformed into vapor (steam) and the vapor is then condensed back into its liquid state.

Also, your home cheese making will regularly require distilled water. There is no substitute. Distilled water is pure H_2O—all of the minerals, treatment chemicals, and impurities have been removed by *distillation*. This is very important because some of those elements—especially the trace chlorine used in tap water—will inhibit or deactivate the enzymes required to make cheese. You can find distilled water in most supermarkets.

Tasty Chatter

For the first recipe, all of the ingredients and each step in the process are critical to the outcome. You can avoid confusion and missed steps by reading all the steps more than once prior to attempting the recipe. It is not a difficult recipe, however. Aside from learning to use new ingredients and process controls, the important lesson here is organization. Start by making a copy of the instructions to work from.

One-Hour Mozzarella

Mozzarella is one of the most fascinating cheeses you can make. The change in the milk is visible and dramatic. The finished cheese literally forms in your hands.

You may encounter problems with your first batch of mozzarella. This is to be expected. It is a simple recipe but a complicated process. Troubleshooting tips are provided after the recipe. There are many things that can go wrong, and cheese making is subject to the snowball effect: problems or mistakes early in the process will be magnified later.

Ingredients:

½ tsp. calcium chloride solution

½ cup distilled water (approximate)

2 tsp. citric acid

½ rennet tablet

½ tsp. flaked salt

1 gallon whole milk

Equipment:

4 small cups or bowls

Cheese pot

Mixing spoon

Ladle or sieve

Microwave oven

Microwave-safe bowl

Yield: *1 pound*	
Cook time: 50 minutes	

1. Ensure your success by preparing as much of the recipe as you can before introducing milk. Begin by premeasuring and preparing the other ingredients. Place the 4 small cups in a row on the counter near your stove. Start at your left and work with each cup as directed in the following bullets.

   ◆ Cup 1: Combine ½ teaspoon calcium chloride with 2 tablespoons distilled water.

Cheese Bite _____

Technically, a 30 percent calcium chloride solution is already diluted. The additional liquid used here is to extend the volume of total liquid and aid in the even distribution throughout the milk.

♦ Cup 2: Measure out citric acid.

♦ Cup 3: Place rennet in the cup and break up with a dry spoon. Add 4 tablespoons distilled water. Stir to help rennet dissolve.

♦ Cup 4: Measure out ½ teaspoon flaked salt.

Cheese Bite

All dry forms of rennet must be rehydrated in distilled water just prior to use. The ratio of ½ tablet to 4 tablespoons water is a useful one, based on experience. You should consult the manufacturer's instructions for your specific rennet supply. Once hydrated, the rennet is ready for use and cannot be stored for later use.

Liquid rennet must also have its volume extended with distilled water for the same reasons as calcium chloride.

2. Place milk into cheese pot and warm over medium heat. It is important to heat milk slowly. Stir in diluted calcium chloride from cup 1. Next, sprinkle in citric acid from cup 2 while gently stirring. Heat slowly until milk reaches 88°F, stirring every few minutes to prevent scorching milk on the bottom of the pot. You will begin to see curds develop.

Whey Watch

Too much stirring of rennet may prevent curds from knitting back together in later recipe steps.

3. Once milk reaches 88°F, add diluted rennet mixture from cup 3. Gently stir in with an up-and-down motion for 1 to 2 minutes. Then stir only briefly every couple minutes to distribute the heat, until milk reaches 105°F. You will see the rennet's effect very clearly as it breaks the protein bond with water and forces the full separation of curds from whey.

4. When milk reaches 105°F, remove the pot from heat. Cover and allow milk to rest for 20 minutes. Do not agitate the pot during this time, and do not peek. This rest period allows the acid and rennet to retrieve as much firm curd as the milk is capable of providing.

5. Open the pot—you will find a white mass of curds floating in the surrounding greenish liquid whey. Use a slotted spoon or strainer to transfer curds to a microwave-safe dish. If curds are too soft to transfer, let milk set a few more minutes.

Avoid collecting whey as you extract curds. It is fine to pour off excess whey as you go. Gently press curds together with the spoon to force out as much whey as possible. There is no reason to hurry, provided curd stays warm.

6. Place curds into the microwave and cook on high for 1 minute. Heating curds will cause them to contract and expel more whey.

7. Remove the dish from the microwave; press curds again with your spoon, forcing out more whey. Begin to knead curd mass with the spoon, as you would bread dough, to distribute heat evenly. Add flaked salt from cup 4 a little at a time as you mix. The cheese should begin to mass together and become sticky.

8. Place curds back into the microwave and heat on high for 1 minute. Remove from the microwave and drain any remaining whey. This time cheese may be too hot to handle, at 140°F to 150°F.

9. Knead cheese with your spoon again until it sticks to the spoon and pulls away from the bowl. Cheese will begin to look glossy. Keep kneading, pulling, and stretching until cheese cools and ribs form as you pull on it. When it begins to stretch like taffy, it is almost done. All the stirring and stretching is done so the entire mass of cheese cools at the same rate.

10. Place finished cheese in an airtight container or wrap in plastic wrap and refrigerate. Use cheese within 1 week or store in the freezer for up to 1 month. If your cheese is too soft to shred for pizza, place it in the freezer for a short time, then shred and use partly frozen.

> **Whey Watch**
>
> Not all microwaves are equal! If the cheese does not mass together, you will need to leave it in the microwave longer. It will not hurt to increase your microwave time by 10 to 15 seconds, or even more if necessary. Note the total time needed for future reference.

Tasty Chatter

One-Hour Mozzarella is not meant to be aged and should be eaten within 1 week. Commercially prepared mozzarella cheese uses the biological acidification method and is formulated differently than homemade. Its process takes 6 to 7 hours and the cheese then undergoes 1 to 3 weeks of aging, which improves its flavor and melting properties.

Troubleshooting Mozzarella Problems

The following is a list of some common problems with making mozzarella and the possible causes and remedies.

Symptom: The curds don't separate from the whey after adding rennet.

♦ A contaminant has been inadvertently introduced into the milk. If distilled water was not used, chlorine may have deactivated the rennet. Also, check your equipment handling. Residual detergent or sanitizer on utensils may be the problem.

♦ It is possible that your store-bought milk is ultrapasteurized, or your raw milk may have been overheated.

♦ You may have prepared your ingredients too early. This is especially important when preparing rennet tablets.

Symptom: The curds do not mass together after microwaving.

♦ Your source of milk was overheated during pasteurization. Switch brands of milk.

♦ The curds may not be getting hot enough in your microwave. One-minute increments work well with our test kitchen unit, which is 850 watts, but you may have to adjust the time for your particular microwave. The curd mass needs to get to 140°F to 150°F in order to stretch. The cheese requires kneading in order to distribute this temperature throughout the curds.

♦ The milk was over-agitated (stirred) after adding the rennet. This can cause cleavage to take place too soon and too quickly, resulting in a portion of fat escaping capture in the matrix and the collection of water in the curd structure. When you stir continuously, you are actually cutting the curd into small pieces and preventing the formation of a strong matrix.

Symptom: The cheese breaks instead of stretching.

♦ The curds contain too much whey. This is common when the milk you use has been pasteurized at a high temperature. Look for a supplier of the cream-line milk described in Chapter 2. You can also try draining the curds in a mesh strainer for a few minutes to get rid of as much whey as possible before microwaving them.

♦ The cheese isn't warm enough to stretch.

Whey Watch

The One-Hour Mozzarella recipe is designed specifically for 1 gallon of whole milk. You can't double or divide a cheese-making recipe as you would other recipes. Cheese-making ingredients cause reactions in the milk, and multiplying or dividing them may not give you the desired results. For example, by doubling the rennet, the curds will form faster, but you will not get more curd and excess rennet will make the cheese bitter.

The volume of milk and resulting curd is also an issue. The increased or decreased volume will completely change the thermodynamics of the process. This means that a completely new set of process times and controls are required.

Symptom: The finished cheese wouldn't melt.

◆ This is a common problem with mozzarella made from store-bought milk. The reason has to do with the amount of bound calcium in the milk. The acidity of the milk affects the amount of calcium that remains after the curds are separated. Depending on what type of milk you are using, you may choose to experiment with reducing the amount of calcium chloride used. This may provide softer curd that melts better but is a little harder to stretch.

You can use your fresh mozzarella just as you would the everyday store-bought kind, but as the cheesemaker you should take advantage of the opportunity to liven it up! You can utilize the physical properties of a cheese-in-process to add flavors, aromas, textures, and presentations that are yours alone. Following are a few ideas to get you started.

Flavored Mozzarella

At the point in the process where the salt is added, you can add any other dry ingredients you like. The important thing is that they be dry. Adding liquids or oils will ruin the cheese. One or two teaspoons of crushed red pepper flakes will heat things up. Give the cheese a Southwest kick with crushed dried ancho peppers and chipotles. Chopped sun-dried tomatoes are a great addition, too. Adding about 1 tablespoon of your favorite dip seasoning will create a delicious appetizer that can be served cold or sliced and toasted on crackers under the broiler. Check the ingredients of premixed spices for salt to avoid oversalting the cheese.

Mozzarella Tomato Caprese

The soft, pliable nature of homemade mozzarella provides all kinds of possibilities. This is my favorite. After kneading your mozzarella, pinch off walnut-sized pieces. Take a grape tomato and surround it with the piece of mozzarella. Pinch the cheese together to seal it. Let the cheese firm up in the refrigerator for 1 hour prior to serving. Slice the tomato-stuffed cheeses in half and place on a green salad. Drizzle with extra-virgin olive oil, freshly cracked black pepper, and a generous garnish of fresh basil. You can also serve the capreses whole, in seasoned olive oil, as a surprise appetizer.

Mozzarella tomato caprese.

Traditional-Style Ricotta

You can use the whey from a batch of mozzarella to make a fresh ricotta cheese, but you will need to make it as soon as possible because the whey will begin to spoil within about 2 hours.

Ingredients:

Fresh whey from a batch of mozzarella

½ gallon whole milk

2 to 4 TB. fresh lemon juice or white vinegar

¼ tsp. flaked salt (optional)

Equipment:

Cheese pot

Slotted spoon or strainer

Heatproof bowl

Yield: *1½ to 2 cups*

Cook time: 10 minutes

Drain time: 10 minutes

1. Heat whey to 195°F. Do not let it boil. Whey will go from nearly clear to very cloudy.

2. Add milk to whey. Slowly stir mixture until it returns to 195°F. Curds will float to the top. When the target temperature is reached, remove the cheese pot from heat.

3. Use a slotted spoon or strainer to ladle curds from the pot into a heatproof bowl. Continue until you've removed all the curds you can.

4. Stir in fresh lemon juice or vinegar, 1 tablespoon at a time. Do this until all acid is used or until more curds are floating on top of whey. Skim off new curds and place them in the bowl.

5. Use cheese immediately or refrigerate for up to 3 days. To season ricotta, place cheese in a bowl and mix in flaked salt. For a drier, textured ricotta, place cheese in a *ricotta basket* or cheesecloth-lined colander. Gently break up curds with your hands and allow them to drain into a bowl or sink for 5 to 10 minutes. Cover and store salted cheese in the refrigerator for use within 1 week.

def•i•ni•tion

A **ricotta basket** is a small (about 1 pint), inexpensive, disposable draining mold that allows ricotta curds to drain and dry. It then serves as the packaging for delivering the cheese to the customer.

Lemon Ricotta Poppy Seed Muffins

This is a moist, tangy muffin that can be served for breakfast or afternoon tea.

Yield: *12 muffins*

Prep time: 15 minutes

Cook time: 20 minutes

Ingredients:

2 cups all-purpose flour

½ tsp. baking powder

½ tsp. baking soda

½ tsp. salt

2 TB. poppy seeds

½ cup unsalted butter, room temp.

1 cup sugar

1 TB. lemon zest

1 cup whole-milk ricotta cheese

1 large egg

1 TB. lemon juice

1 tsp. vanilla extract

4 to 6 TB. milk

Tasty Chatter

Ricotta is a popular ingredient in lasagna, manicotti, and cheesecake. In this recipe, the tangy cheese is balanced by the sweetness of the muffin.

---

1. Preheat oven to 350°F and line 12 muffin cups with paper liners.

2. Whisk flour, baking powder, baking soda, salt, and poppy seeds together in a medium bowl.

3. In a larger bowl, mix butter, sugar, and lemon zest together until light. Beat in ricotta until smooth. Add egg, lemon juice, and vanilla and beat until combined. Add dry ingredients and stir in or beat on low speed just until combined. Batter will be very thick. Stir in enough milk to get a batter that you can spoon into the muffin cups.

4. Divide batter among muffin cups. Sprinkle with additional sugar if you like. Bake until pale golden on top, about 20 to 25 minutes.

The Least You Need to Know

◆ Rennet and calcium chloride are needed to make mozzarella cheese.

◆ Mozzarella cheese can be made in 1 hour.

◆ Cheese recipes cannot be multiplied or divided.

◆ Ricotta is actually a cheese by-product since it is made from whey.

Chapter **6**

Culture-Ripened Fresh Cheeses

In This Chapter

◆ The use of starter cultures to make soft cheeses

◆ The combined use of culture and rennet

◆ Homemade draining and shaping molds

◆ Goat's milk versus cow's milk

The cheeses in the previous chapter were created using a selection of different acids added directly to the milk. In this chapter, we will use bacteria (starter cultures) to convert lactose to lactic acid, a process described in Chapter 2. The advantage of this all-natural bacterial acidification method is that a portion of the bacteria remains with the curd after separation. This carryover culture will continue to develop lactic acid as the cheese matures. More importantly, the active cultures generate flavor compounds that make the cheese much more interesting and complex on the taste buds. Starter cultures also contribute to the texture and mouthfeel of the finished cheese.

Making Bacteria-Acidified Cheese

In the following recipes, we will make bacteria-acidified cheese. You can use freeze-dried direct-to-vat mesophilic starter culture or active-culture buttermilk to inoculate the milk. Unlike the yogurt used in previous recipes, which contains *Lactobacillus delbrueckii* ssp. *bulgaricus* as its primary starter, buttermilk will provide *Lactococcus lactis* ssp. *lactis* and *cremoris*, the primary lactic acid–producing strain used for cheese making, and a secondary culture called *biovar diacetylactis*, which produces *diacetyl* flavors.

def•i•ni•tion

Diacetyl is a compound which has a sweet aroma and the flavor of buttery cream. In cheese, it is best described as the body and pleasant richness that lingers after the cheese is swallowed.

In years past, buttermilk referred solely to the liquid that remained after cream was churned into butter. The liquid from cultured butter (butter made from ripened cream) was used to inoculate milk for cheese making. Modern buttermilk is actually a cultured dairy product made directly from milk. When purchasing buttermilk for use as a cheese starter, be sure the carton states "active culture," and look for the freshest one available.

Cheese Bite

When shopping for dairy products, take along a cooler with some ice in it. Place the dairy goods and any other perishables in the cooler for the trip home so they remain as fresh as possible. You never know when you will be sidetracked.

Preparing a Weak Rennet Solution

The batch sizes in this chapter are small, due to the limited shelf life of the fresh cheeses being made. A special preparation of weak rennet solution must be used to force coagulation. This is necessary due to the smaller yield of the recipes. Any excess application of rennet will cause the cheese to be bitter.

Prepare the weak rennet solution by completely dissolving ¼ rennet tablet in 4 tablespoons distilled water. Each recipe will call for a set amount of this solution. A new weak solution must be made for each recipe unless recipes are being made simultaneously. Discard any unused portion since it will not keep.

If you are using rennet in liquid form, the recipes will give the exact amount in drops to be used.

Crème Fraîche

Crème fraîche is the Old World version of sour cream. The texture is lighter and the flavor is less tart than its North American counterpart.

Ingredients:

1 qt. light cream

1 TB. active-culture buttermilk or ⅛ tsp. mesophilic culture

1½ tsp. weak rennet solution (see previous page) or 1 drop liquid rennet diluted in 2 TB. distilled water

Equipment:

Saucepan

Measuring spoons

Thermometer

Spoon

½ yard fine cheesecloth (optional)

Yield: *Up to 1 quart, depending on thickness desired*	
Prep time: 15 minutes **Rest time:** 12 hours	

1. Heat cream to 86°F in a stainless steel saucepan over low to medium-low heat. It will take very little time for this to happen, so stand by.

2. Remove warm cream from heat and stir in buttermilk or mesophilic culture. (If you are using mesophilic culture, wait 2 minutes for freeze-dried crystals to dissolve before continuing.)

3. Add weak rennet solution and gently stir for 1 minute with an up-and-down motion.

4. Cover the pot and let cream ripen at room temperature for 12 hours or overnight.

5. You should now have a thick, sour cream consistency with a creamy, slightly tart flavor. If it is not as thick as you would like, place cheese in a strainer lined with double thickness cheesecloth and allow to drain until the texture suits your taste.

6. Place in an airtight container and store refrigerated for up to 1 week.

def•i•ni•tion

Crème fraîche originated in the Brittany and Normandy regions of France. It is traditionally made by setting aside fresh cream and allowing the natural lactic bacteria to create the thick, smooth, tart product. In the interest of consistency, the inoculation method used here is preferred.

Crème fraîche is a staple of French cuisine. It makes a great topping for fresh berries and is used in many dessert applications. It is similar in texture and flavor to sour cream but with the added advantage of holding up to cooking processes better. This makes it a good ingredient in savory dishes as well.

Berry Crème Fraîche Crisp

A sweet berry mixture gets a surprise topping of tangy crème fraîche. It's all topped off with a crumbly, buttery oat topping.

Yield: *6 ½-cup servings*

Prep time: 15 minutes

Cook time: 30 minutes

Ingredients:

4 cups fresh or frozen mixed berries (raspberries, blackberries, and blueberries in any combination)

1½ cups flour

¼ cup sugar

½ tsp. cinnamon

1 cup crème fraîche

½ cup brown sugar

½ tsp. salt

½ cup rolled oats

½ cup cold butter cut into cubes

1. Preheat oven to 375°F.

2. Toss berries with ½ cup flour, sugar, and cinnamon and pour into an 8×8 baking dish. Spread crème fraîche evenly over top of berries.

3. Mix brown sugar, remaining 1 cup flour, salt, and oats together. Cut cold butter into mixture by hand or pulse in using a food processor until topping is crumbly. Spoon topping over filling. Bake in the oven for 30 minutes or until topping is golden brown.

Golden Potato Gratin

The flavors of milk, cream, and potatoes are blended with aromatic herbs to create a simple side dish. The use of crème fraîche instead of traditional cheese is an unexpected twist.

Ingredients:

1½ cups crème fraîche

⅓ cup heavy cream

3 lb. Russet or Yukon Gold potatoes, peeled and sliced ⅛ inch thick

1½ tsp. coarse salt

¾ tsp. black pepper

1½ tsp. dried rosemary

Garlic powder or granules (optional)

Yield: *8 ½-cup servings*
Prep time: 30 minutes
Cook time: 1 hour

1. Preheat oven to 400°F. Butter bottom and sides of a 13×9 baking pan.

2. Whisk together crème fraîche and cream.

3. Arrange ⅓ potato slices evenly in the bottom of the baking pan. Sprinkle with ½ teaspoon salt, ¼ teaspoon pepper, and ½ teaspoon rosemary. Lightly sprinkle with garlic (if using), then spread ⅓ crème fraîche mixture over potatoes. Repeat layering two more times.

4. Bake for 30 minutes. Reduce temperature to 350°F and bake another 25 to 30 minutes or until potatoes are tender and top is golden brown.

Neufchâtel

The soft texture of *Neufchâtel* makes it an excellent spread for bagels, and it substitutes very well in recipes calling for cream cheese.

Yield: *1½ to 2 pounds*

Prep time: 20 minutes

Rest time: 20 hours minimum

Ingredients:

1 gallon whole milk

1 pint heavy cream

½ tsp. calcium chloride dissolved in 2 TB. distilled water

2 TB. active-culture buttermilk or ⅛ tsp. mesophilic culture

2 tsp. weak rennet solution or 1 drop liquid rennet diluted in 2 TB. distilled water

1 tsp. flaked salt (optional)

Equipment:

Cheese pot

Slotted spoon

1 yard fine cheesecloth

Colander or strainer

Measuring spoons

1. Combine milk, heavy cream, and diluted calcium chloride in a stainless steel pot. Heat mixture to 86°F over medium-low heat, stirring occasionally to distribute heat evenly.

2. Remove the pot from heat and stir in buttermilk or mesophilic culture.

3. Add weak rennet solution and gently stir in with an up-and-down motion for 1 minute.

4. Cover and let milk ripen at room temperature for 12 hours or overnight.

def•i•ni•tion

Neufchâtel is a soft, unripened cow's milk cheese that originates from the city of Neufchâtel in the Normandy region of France, where it is often found molded into different shapes. It is similar to American cream cheese except for the fat content. Neufchâtel has less fat, since it is made mostly with whole milk as opposed to heavy cream.

5. There should now be some curd separation from the whey. Carefully tip the pot into a sink to discard as much of the whey as possible without disturbing the curds. It is important that you do not break up the curd mass.

6. Line a large colander or strainer with a double thickness of fine cheesecloth at least 18×18. Use a slotted spoon or small strainer to gently transfer curds to the cheesecloth. Let curds drain for 30 minutes.

7. Gather cheesecloth corners together to form a draining bag and hang cheese over the bowl or a sink to catch whey. Make sure you use a bowl large enough to collect up to 2 quarts of whey. Hang bag to drain for 12 hours or overnight.

Hanging cheese bag with a bowl below to catch the whey as it drips.

8. Discard collected whey and place cheese in a bowl. Knead cheese with a spoon until it develops a pastelike texture. Add flaked salt (if using) plus any herbs you like. Neufchâtel can be placed in any shape mold you desire, or just cover and refrigerate.

Vegetable Dill Cheese Spread

Neufchâtel blends well with a variety of ingredients to create tasty spreads and dips. Use any number of combinations of herbs and vegetables to your liking.

Yield: *18 to 20 1-ounce servings*
Prep time: 20 minutes

Ingredients:

16 oz. Neufchâtel cheese

2 TB. finely chopped carrot

2 TB. finely chopped green pepper

2 TB. finely chopped radish

2 TB. finely chopped red onion

1 tsp. dill weed

½ tsp. fresh ground black pepper

½ tsp. salt

Mix all ingredients together and use as a spread on bagels, vegetables, or crackers.

Tasty Chatter
This is a savory and creamy spread for crackers, celery, or bagels. The vegetable and herb combinations are endless, and chopped dried fruit and honey could easily substitute for the vegetables and dill.

Easy Fruit Tart

Sweet berries are complemented by the slightly tart Neufchâtel cheese. The flaky puff pastry adds to the contrast of textures in this pretty dessert.

Ingredients:

1 frozen puff pastry sheet

8 oz. Neufchâtel cheese

⅓ cup powdered sugar

2 TB. apple juice

3 cups assorted berries

2 TB. apricot jam, melted then cooled

Yield: *12 3-inch square servings*
Prep time: 60 minutes
Cook time: 20 minutes

1. Preheat oven to 400°F.

2. Thaw pastry according to package directions. Unfold on a lightly floured surface and roll into 14×10-inch rectangle. Place on a large baking sheet and form a rim by wetting edges with water and folding them toward the center by ½ inch. Press edges firmly in place and pierce all over pastry with a fork. Blind bake by placing pie weights or dried beans on a piece of foil cut to fit inside bottom of pastry. Bake at 400°F for 15 to 20 minutes or until golden brown. Cool completely on wire rack. Carefully remove foil and weights.

3. Either by hand or with a mixer, beat Neufchâtel, sugar, and apple juice in medium-size bowl until smooth. Spread evenly onto the cooled pastry.

4. Place berries decoratively over the cheese layer. Brush melted jam lightly over berries and chill until ready to serve. Cut into 12 squares for serving.

Molded Cheese Rounds

These individual rounds of simple fresh-ripened cheese are perfect as single-size servings paired with sweet jam or jelly and warm toast. They also make a savory afternoon snack when topped with hot pepper jelly and served with a large soft pretzel.

Yield: *4 2-oz. cheese rounds*

Prep time: 3 hours 15 minutes

Ingredients:

2 qt. whole milk

4 TB. active-culture butter-milk

¼ rennet tablet prepared in distilled water

2 tsp. flaked salt

Equipment:

Double boiler

Skimmer or sieve

Whisk

Small serving spoon

Plastic food wrap

8 9-oz. Dixie-style cups made of waxed paper

1 pointed skewer or a knitting needle

Draining mat with catch tray

Zip-lock bags (sandwich size)

Drinking straw

Tasty Chatter

This recipe introduces you to the use of shaping and draining molds. There are a number of shaping molds used by cheese-makers. Some are designed to make certain cheese styles and others are mere whimsy. In the Molded Cheese Rounds recipe, you are going to make your own draining molds using house-hold items. This same technique can be used in subsequent recipes, or you may choose to purchase the specific molds ascribed to the cheese.

---

1. Make a set of disposable draining molds by using a long skewer or knitting needle to poke holes in 4 of the paper cups. Push the skewer through the walls and bottom from the inside out. The holes should be about the size of a pencil lead. Line up the molds in a row on a draining mat placed in a container to collect the whey.

Cheese molds made of waxed paper cups.

2. Place the bottom of a double boiler with about 2 inches of water on the stove and bring to a slow boil or simmer. Place the top of the boiler over simmering water and add milk.

3. Remove the double boiler from heat and stir milk. Residual heat from the simmering water will warm milk. When milk reaches 86°F, stir in buttermilk or mesophilic starter. Continue stirring for 20 to 30 seconds.

4. Remove the bowl of milk from the double boiler, cover with plastic wrap, and leave milk to ripen for 60 minutes.

5. Gently stir in prepared rennet for 20 to 30 seconds. Re-cover the bowl with plastic wrap and let milk rest for 60 minutes. Milk will form into one solid curd mass. If you gently press the backs of your fingers into the top of the curd mass near the side of the bowl, it will "give" without breaking like a soft-set gelatin. There should be a small amount of whey visible around the edge of the bowl when you do this.

6. Use a wire whisk to gently push through curd mass and then lift out. Do this over entire surface of curd mass. Then pull the whisk horizontally through curd mass, making a tic-tac-toe pattern. Do not repeatedly run the whisk back and

forth. Once in each direction—covering the total surface once—is enough. Allow curds to set for 5 minutes.

7. While curds are resting, bring water in the double boiler back to a boil then remove from heat.

8. Place bowl of curds back on top of the double boiler and stir very gently until whey reaches 100°F. This will take about 5 to 8 minutes. Do not let the curd exceed 102°F. Remove bowl from double boiler and let curds settle for 5 minutes.

9. Curds will now have settled to the bottom of the bowl. Carefully pour off as much whey as you can without losing curds. Use a slotted spoon or strainer to hold back curds as you tip the bowl and allow whey to slowly drain off.

10. Add flaked salt to drained curds and gently mix in.

11. Using a skimmer or sieve, scoop up some curds. Use a smaller spoon to fill the draining cups. Divide curds evenly between the 4 perforated cup molds.

12. Fill the remaining 4 whole cups about ⅔ full with water and place 1 whole cup directly on top of each mold cup. The water will act as your cheese press. Allow curds to press for 15 minutes.

13. Discard whey collected in the draining tray. Remove the water cups and gently tap out cheese rounds from their molds. Turn cheese rounds over and place them back into their molds. Place the water cups back on top of curds and press for another 15 minutes. Remove collected whey as necessary.

14. Repeat the "turning" process in step 13, but this time leave cheese to press overnight. Place a piece of coarse cheese-cloth over the top to keep pests away.

15. The next day, remove and discard the water cups. You'll see that each cheese has been reduced to a small disk 1 to 1½ inches thick. Tap out cheeses and discard the molds. (You may find you have to cut away the molds if they have become saturated with whey.)

16. Place a dry draining mat on a tray and set cheese rounds on it. Cover with coarse cheesecloth and allow cheeses to air dry. Depending on humidity, this will take from 1 hour to 1 day.

17. When edges of cheeses begin to form a rind (the rind will appear more yellow than the rest of the cheese), wrap and store cheeses. Cheeses are alive and need to be protected from exposure to air. You will need a zip-lock bag for each cheese and a drinking straw. Place 1 cheese into each bag. Insert straw into the bag at one edge. Zip bag closed until it contacts the straw. Use your mouth to suck all of the air out of the bag, then slip the straw out and close zipper completely. The best place to keep cheese is the vegetable crisper of your refrigerator. They should store well in your refrigerator for up to 1 month.

Cheese Bite

Every week, evaluate one of your cheese rounds. Unwrap a cheese and place it on a drying mat. Allow it to come to room temperature. Make notes about its appearance and any apparent changes. Cut a small wedge from it. Smell the cheese and note any aromas given off. Next, taste the wedge of cheese. Keep a small amount of the cheese in your mouth and take a breath through the mouth, exhaling through the nose. This will bring the aroma of the cheese through your nasal passages, which will help you to understand and appreciate both the smell and taste of the cheese. Make notes as you experience the cheese and compare your notes to the previous tasting. Comment on the changes you can identify from week to week.

Chèvre and Fromage Blanc

The next recipe has the distinction of producing two different cheeses based on the type of milk used, goat's or cow's. The recipe and procedures are identical, regardless of milk you use.

Cheese Bite

Goat's milk is interchangeable with cow's milk in most cheese recipes. Cheese made with goat's milk will tend to be tarter than the cow's milk version because of the unique properties of the fat it contains. The curd produced from goat's milk will also be softer.

Saint Maure mold.

The traditional log-shaped chèvre is produced by draining the curd using tall cylindrical molds, named Saint Maure molds. A 1-gallon batch of fresh chèvre will require the use of two Saint Maure draining molds that are 10×2 inches. As the cheese drains and shrinks, it is formed into short logs of about 2 inches in diameter by 4 inches long. Once formed, the cheese may be consumed fresh or allowed to ripen briefly and may develop a bloomy surface mold by the addition of *Penicillium candidum* to the milk. You may choose to acquire the appropriate molds in the future, but for now the cheese can be made by draining the curd in cheesecloth as in the Neufchâtel recipe. Instructions for both methods are provided.

def•i•ni•tion

Penicillium candidum is the mold-producing bacteria that appears as a velvety white rind on the surface of fresh-ripened cheeses, most notably Camembert and Brie.

Chèvre and Fromage Blanc

Chèvre or fromage blanc will range from semi-soft to firm in texture and has a mildly tart flavor that lends itself well to fruits, salads, and desserts. Softer versions make a great spread for breads, too.

Ingredients:

1 gallon whole goat's milk (chèvre) or whole cow's milk (fromage blanc)

½ tsp. liquid calcium chloride in 2 TB. distilled water

2 TB. active-culture buttermilk or ⅛ tsp. mesophilic culture

2 tsp. weak rennet solution or 1 drop liquid rennet diluted in 2 TB. distilled water

1 tsp. flaked salt

Equipment:

Cheese pot

Slotted spoon

1 yard fine cheesecloth

Colander or strainer

Measuring spoons

Saint Maure or other goat cheese draining molds (optional)

Baking pan or tray to collect whey (optional)

Yield: *1½ to 2 pounds*	
Prep time: 15 minutes	
Rest time: 24 hours minimum	

1. Combine milk and diluted calcium chloride in cheese pot. Heat mixture to 86°F over medium-low heat, stirring occasionally to distribute heat evenly.

2. Remove from heat and stir in buttermilk or mesophilic starter.

Tasty Chatter

Around 8000 B.C.E., farmers in the eastern Mediterranean began keeping small herds of goats for meat, hides, and milk. Goats were an easily mobile food supply. In the eighth century, the Saracens came to the west of France and left behind their goats and the recipe for chèvre. In fact, the word *chèvre* is simply French for "goat." For obvious reasons, when this recipe is prepared using cow's milk, the name is changed to fromage blanc.

3. Add rennet solution and gently stir in with an up-and-down motion for 1 minute.

4. Cover and let milk ripen at room temperature for 12 hours or overnight.

5. There should now be some curd separation from whey. Curd mass will be soft and custardlike in texture. Carefully tip pot into sink to discard as much whey as possible without disturbing curds.

6a. Draining Option 1: Cheesecloth—Line a large colander with a double thickness of fine cheesecloth. Use a slotted spoon or small strainer to transfer curds to cheesecloth. Gather cheesecloth corners together to form a draining bag. Hang cheese over the bowl or sink to drain for at least 12 hours or overnight.

    Discard collected whey and place cheese in the bowl. Sprinkle flaked salt over cheese and gently mix in. Store your fresh chèvre in an airtight container in the refrigerator for up to 2 weeks.

6b. Draining Option 2: Molds—Place the molds you'll be using into a baking pan or tray to catch whey. After draining curds in a cheesecloth bag overnight, open the bag and gently scoop curds into the molds. Remove whey that collects in the box periodically during the day.

Whey Watch

Predraining the curd in cheesecloth may be necessary when store-bought milk is used. If you are using low-temperature pasteurized milk or raw milk that you have pasteurized yourself, you may be able to drain the curd using only the cheese-draining molds mentioned here. This is the traditional filling method—the curds are ladled into molds and allowed to drain. More curds are added to each mold as room becomes available. This is done until all of the curd has been placed in the molds. The curds are set to drain for two days, during which the cheese is turned twice to promote even drainage.

Let curds continue to drain for another 24 hours in the molds or until cheese is firm enough to be removed from the molds and hold its shape. When you are ready to unmold cheese, invert the mold and give it a firm rap on a clean surface. Do this until cheese releases. Wrap your cheese in plastic wrap and store in the refrigerator for up to 2 weeks.

~

Herbed Cheese Spread

This spread will be slightly softer and tangier than the Vegetable Dill Cheese Spread made with Neufchâtel. Any mix of fresh or dried herbs will work.

Ingredients:

1 cup fresh chèvre

1 to 2 TB. favorite fresh herb blend or 1 to 2 tsp. dried herbs

Yield: *8 1-ounce servings*
Prep time: 5 minutes

Option 1: Mix herbs into fresh chèvre. For best results, refrigerate overnight to allow the flavors to blend.

Option 2: Cover the outside of your molded cheese logs with minced, fresh herbs before sealing it in plastic wrap.

Pasta with Tomatoes, Chèvre, and Basil

A simple entrée or side dish, this pasta is tossed with lightly dressed tomatoes and fresh basil. The fresh chèvre melts, creating a tart, creamy sauce.

> **Yield:** *4 to 6 2-cup entrée servings, or 8 to 12 1-cup side dish servings*
>
> **Prep time:** 15 minutes
>
> **Cook time:** 10 minutes

Ingredients:

1 clove minced garlic

1 TB. quality vinegar

¼ cup virgin olive oil

1 to 2 lb. seeded and diced plum tomatoes

Salt and black pepper

1 lb. dried spiral pasta (such as fusilli or cellentani)

4 oz. fresh chèvre

½ cup sliced fresh basil

1. In a large mixing bowl, combine garlic and vinegar, then whisk in oil. Add tomatoes and season with salt and pepper.

2. Cook pasta according to package directions.

3. Drain pasta and add to the bowl of marinated tomatoes. Add chèvre to hot pasta and toss everything together until cheese melts. Top with basil.

The Least You Need to Know

◆ The primary lactic acid starter culture used for cheese making is called *Lactococcus lactis* ssp. *lactis* and *cremoris*.

◆ Making a weak rennet solution is necessary in smaller batch recipes of cheeses.

◆ Crème fraîche originated in France and is similar to sour cream.

◆ Chèvre can be made with goat's milk or cow's milk (fromage blanc), and can be prepared using cheesecloth or molds.

Part 3

Cultured Cheese and Conventional Cheese Making

It is time to graduate to more complex fresh cheeses. These recipes will require the use of bacterial starters to provide the physical transformation of milk into cheese and create the flavors and aromas that are such a large part of cheese enjoyment. You will learn to use time and patience as processing tools. The cheeses made in this part have many uses, and the recipes for using them will highlight the unique textures and flavors of each.

Chapter 7

The Formal Cheese-Making Process

In This Chapter

- ◆ The steps used in traditional cheese making
- ◆ Proper milk preparation and usage
- ◆ Gel development and processing

To this point you have learned what cheese is made of and worked to understand what happens while making cheese and what causes it to happen. Now you will mold that knowledge into the structured progression of steps used by professional cheesemakers. This detailed application of principles and techniques, along with new ingredients and equipment, will now seem far less alien than it might have in prior chapters.

The Cheesemaker and the Brewer

At first glance, you will find that most cheese-making recipes are very much alike. This is because the basics of all cheese making are dictated by the physical and chemical composition of milk. As mentioned earlier, making cheese and brewing beer are very similar. Both are limited to a small list of ingredients, and each relies on a process rather than simply raw materials to create their unique finished products. After the ingredients are selected, the keys to manufacturing both are temperature and time.

Many of the chemical and biological interactions necessary to make cheese (and beer) will only occur within specific temperature ranges. These interactions also require a set amount of time to reach or complete the desired transformation. Subtle differences in ingredients, temperatures, and timing are what produce the wide variety of cheeses and beers.

def•i•ni•tion

A **baker's formula** is a recipe of ingredients with individual quantities expressed as a percentage of the total weight.

The point here is that cheese making, like brewing, is chemistry and not cooking. You cannot double or divide a cheese or beer recipe as you would cookie dough. Nor will multiplication work as it would with a *baker's formula* for bread dough. The difference is that no matter how large the batch of dough, the individual cookies or bread loaves will remain the same size. However, a batch of cheese is the size of a batch of cheese.

A cheese recipe is actually a procedural formulation of both ingredients and process, designed to produce the desired cheese style from a fixed batch size. The dynamics of this can be mind boggling. Suffice it to say that a change in batch size does not mean that all ingredients will change proportionately, and the process details will most certainly not remain the same. A change in process (with steps either altered or missed) will result in irreparable failure, and there is rarely an opportunity to turn back.

Whey Watch

Using simple multiplication to double a recipe increases the physical mass of the batch, and thus modifies the thermodynamics involved, requiring an adjustment to the ripening process. This then alters the rate of lactic acid production, which affects curd formation and results in an unpredictable flavor and texture in the cheese. Now that's a chain reaction!

Cheese-Making Process Flow

Cheese making is a sequence of events, and each event is dependent on its predecessor. Not all cheeses will require all steps, but the order in which the required steps are performed remains the same. Within each step there will be variations in ingredients, time, and temperature depending on the cheese being made. When a cheese does not require a step, that step is simply skipped, and the flow of the process picks up with the next required step. The process basics of cheese making are listed in Table 7.1.

Table 7.1: The General Process Flow Required to Make Cheese

Process Step	General Description
Standardization	Preparation of the milk for cheese making
Acidification	Either direct acid or inoculation
Coagulation	By acid, rennet, or enzyme
Curd processing	Cutting, cooking, washing
Pressing/shaping	Curd knitting, shaping
Rind preparation	Salting, brining, surface mold application
Aging and curing	Flavor development

The next pages will detail the actions taken within each process step with only a few references to specific cheeses.

Standardization of Cheese Milk

Consistency in cheese making starts with an analysis of the available milk. A cheese can never be better than the milk it is made from. As a comparison, the quality of a bottle of wine is decided on the day the grapes are harvested. The winemaker and cheesemaker have very specific expectations of the condition of their raw materials. They each apply known standards and experience to identify and correct flaws. "Standardizing" the cheese milk means making adjustments to optimize the effects of each process step and maximize the quality of the finished cheese.

If you are using raw milk, we recommend pasteurizing it as described in Chapter 2. This first step in standardization creates a healthy "clean slate" environment where the starter culture will dominate. Once the starter is established, the increase in acidity makes the environment inhospitable to unwanted bacteria. If preexisting bacteria are allowed to establish a foothold prior to inoculation, the effects of the starter may be diminished.

The character of certain cheeses is dependent on the amount of fat available. If the total fat content is not what is expected by the recipe, the formulation may not work. Milk that is too fatty is corrected with the addition of skim milk, provided that the additional water content will not cause a greater problem. Conversely, fat content is increased by adding heavy cream. At first glance, you may think more is better. But in this case that's not true. Adding excessive milkfat to a recipe makes it easier for fat globules to escape the matrix created by the protein when rennet is added.

The quality of a cheese is dependent on the ratio of casein (protein) to milkfat. Milk that is low in protein can be corrected by the addition of skim milk, or nonfat dry milk as a last resort. When nonfat dry milk is used to increase casein, it should be rehydrated in refrigerated skim milk for 24 hours prior to use. This provides time for total hydration and reduces the chance of off flavors from the dry milk showing up in the cheese. Skim milk is used because water alone would dilute the available casein. If the cheese milk will not be heat treated prior to use, the dry milk additive should be processed as described in Chapter 2 in the section "Using Powdered Milk."

You have already used another standardizing technique in previous recipes, which was the addition of calcium chloride to help compensate for the denaturing of protein by pasteurization.

All of this milk chemistry is simplified for the majority of hobby cheesemakers who use store-bought milk. The USDA has established standards for the definition of every dairy product available to consumers. Detailed definitions can be found at www. access.gpo.gov/nara/cfr/waisidx_06/21cfr131_06.html.

Whey Watch

To assure uniform coloring of cheese, annatto must be added directly to the milk during standardization. Annatto has a high pH value (alkalinity), so the use of annatto to color cheese milk will influence the effectiveness of rennet by retarding its ability to cause separation.

Some cheeses may require the addition of ingredients specific to the cheese being made. For example, annatto, also called cheese coloring, is a common additive. Annatto is a yellowish-red dye made from the tropical shrub called achiote (or *Bixa orellana*). Pigment is taken from the pulp around the seeds and processed to make the dye used in food and fabric coloring. Its purpose in cheese making is to mimic the natural color of cheese made from the milk of cows, whose diet is primarily green pasture grasses.

Acidification and Secondary Cultures

Cheese starter culture is added to the milk and allowed to acidify the milk for a period of 30 to 60 minutes. Cheese recipes will provide the specific time required. This period is referred to as ripening the milk. Add the starter culture and gently stir it in with a ladle or large spoon in an up-and-down motion. Be careful not to pump a lot of air into the milk. It will take about 1 to 2 minutes of gentle stirring action to thoroughly distribute the starter.

You must be able to maintain a fixed temperature during the ripening phase. The recipe will indicate an appropriate range for the cheese being made. You must avoid hot and cold spots inside the cheese pot for the duration of the ripening period. Unless a recipe instructs you to stir at this time, the cheese milk should be kept still. The best method for holding a constant temperature is to place the cheese pot into a water bath of the desired temperature. If the rest period is less than 60 minutes, and the *ambient temperature* is not overly cool, this will work without any fuss. For periods between 1 and 2 hours, you will need to monitor the temperature of the bath water, adding more hot water as needed.

Whey Watch

Special attention must be paid to sanitation during the ripening stage. The milk will be in a temperature danger zone for an extended period of time, offering airborne bacteria a nice home. Milk that has not been properly pasteurized may also contain unwanted bacteria causing excessive acid and carbon dioxide production.

def•i•ni•tion

The term **ambient temperature** refers to the temperature of the environment in the area surrounding an object.

Dairy products like yogurt that rely on acid production for coagulation require ripening at warmer temperatures for 2 hours or more. These may require mechanical help in holding the target temperature. An electrical device called a brew belt or heat belt can be wrapped around the water bath vessel or directly around the cheese pot. When plugged in, this device will maintain a preset temperature, thus keeping the cheese milk warm. You can also try using a small heating pad to warm the water bath vessel.

During this ripening stage, the bacteria in the starter culture will begin to consume the lactose in the warm milk and produce lactic acid. The lactic acid will then begin the separation of curds and whey. The production of lactic acid is greatly influenced by temperature. Recipes that require more acid production may call for warmer temperatures, more time, or both. Cheeses that require very quick acid production may call for a combination of starter cultures, such as *Lactobacillus helveticus* used in conjunction with *Streptococcus thermophilus* to increase the rate of acid production in Italian cheese styles.

Certain cheese styles require additional cultures and/or enzymes to generate the character traits that make the cheese unique. These are called secondary cultures (see Table 7.2). A prime example is *Propionic shermanii*, the bacteria used to produce the large volume of carbon dioxide gas required to create eyes in cheese. It also produces propionic and acetic acids that give the distinctive flavor associated with Alpine-style cheese.

Table 7.2: Secondary Cheese Cultures and Cheeses They Produce

Secondary Cultures	Manifestation	Cheeses
Propionic shermanii	Flavor, eyes	Swiss, Gruyere
Penicillium roqueforti	Blue veins, flavor	Stilton, Roquefort
Penicillium candidum	White bloom, flavor	Brie, Camembert
Brevibacterium linens	Red smear, aroma	Limburger, Muenster
Other Additives		
Lipase enzyme powder	Sharpness	Romano, Provolone

In addition to secondary cultures, there is a collection of enzymes and other additives used to create distinctive flavors. It is not unusual for a cheese to require a combination of secondary cultures and enzymes. In many cases one will help to create the optimal environment for the other to flourish. Any recipe calling for secondary cultures or enzymes will include detailed descriptions of the additive's purpose and how it is to be used.

Coagulation and Gel Development

Rennet, as described in Chapter 2, is added to acidified milk to coagulate (solidify) the milk protein into a solid curd. Rennet should be diluted in cool, distilled water before adding it to the milk. This will help to distribute the enzyme quickly and evenly, assuring consistent gel formation. When adding rennet to the milk, stir gently in an up-and-down motion for 1 minute. Do not stir vigorously. Excessive agitation will interfere with the development of the protein network and result in loose or fragmented curd.

The formation of a solid curd mass by rennet is sometimes called "setting" because the physical transformation is similar to the firming of a liquid into a gelatin or pudding state. In cheese making, the solid collection of protein and fat is called a gel. The firmness of the gel, just like the development of lactic acid, is a function of time and temperature. The temperature can be controlled using the same methods described for ripening. The initial coagulation can appear to be quick and complete after only a few minutes, but the process of gel development will continue for a longer period of time.

Individual recipes will specify the conditions needed for the cheese you are making. Full gel development will take 30 to 60 minutes. If it takes longer than 75 minutes, first reconsider the type of milk you are using and how it was pasteurized. Secondly, examine your procedure for preparing the rennet solution. (Chapter 2 covers both milk and rennet extensively.) After that, consider replacing your rennet supply if it has weakened with time. As a last resort, you may add slightly more rennet the next time you make your recipe.

The cheese milk must remain undisturbed during gel development. Any breaking up of the gel mass will cause the resulting curds to shrink or fragment. This may result in curds that are inappropriate for the style of cheese being made. The greatest danger here is the premature loss of moisture, resulting in curds that will not bond later and a cheese that will easily crumble due to having less moisture than intended.

When you add the prepared rennet to the cheese milk, you must note the time. You can then check the progress of gel development by floating a lightweight food storage container (such as a small empty margarine tub) on top of the milk. By gently pushing the container you will see that it easily glides across the surface. Once the milk begins to "set," marking the onset of *flocculation*, the container will remain stationary on the surface as if it is stuck to the milk. Note the time when this happens. You can now determine the flocculation time to be the minutes since you added the rennet. To estimate when gel development will be complete, multiply the flocculation time by the rate factor from Table 7.3 listed for the cheese style being made. For example: If it took 10 minutes for the onset of flocculation and the rate factor is 3, the gel would be ready to process 30 minutes (3×10) from the time the rennet was added.

def•i•ni•tion

Flocculation is the precipitation of suspended solids out of a liquid—in this case, curds from whey.

Table: 7.3: Rate Factors for Estimating Gel Development Time

Cheese or Style	Factor
Alpine, Swiss, Parmesan, Romano	2–2.5
Cheddar, Gouda, Havarti, Provolone	3–3.5
Feta, Blue	4
Brie, Camembert	5–6

Source: American Farmstead Cheese by Kinstedt

Note that the smaller a factor is, the softer the curd will be and the firmer the cheese will be. Higher factor numbers result in firmer curd but softer cheese. Sounds backward, right? The reason is that firm curd will be less willing to give up moisture later on.

Cheese Bite

You can also determine the onset of flocculation by inserting a curd knife into the milk, withdrawing it slowly, and observing when curd particles are present in the milk flowing off the blade.

Testing the completeness of gel formation is done by checking for a "clean break." This simple test involves inserting a flat blade like a curd knife diagonally into the gel and gently prying it up. The clean break is demonstrated on the surface as a split or crack which remains open, leaving a permanent scar on the surface of the gel. The clean break will be most defined when using raw or low-temperature pasteurized milk. When performed on standard pasteurized milk (most store-bought milk), the surface break may show signs of closing up or healing within a few minutes. A well-developed gel will resemble poached egg white.

Curd Processing

Once gel development is complete and a clean break is achieved, the curd is ready to be processed. Processing begins with cutting the gel into uniform pieces. After that, there may be one or more additional curd processing steps necessary to prepare the curds to make the desired cheese.

Cutting and Healing the Gel

The purpose of cutting the gel into equal-size pieces is to control the draining of whey from within. Cutting the gel into curds increases the exposed surface area, providing more places for the whey to escape. Individual cheese recipes will indicate the specific curd size required for the style of cheese being made. It will be impossible to make all of the curd pieces the same size, but try to make them as uniform as possible.

Cutting the gel into curds.

Cut the curd with a curd knife (see Chapter 3). Insert the blade into the gel and then draw it through the curd mass. Slice the curd from left to right into the required-size slices as indicated in the recipe. Turn the pot 90 degrees and once again cut the curd from left to right, creating a grid pattern. This will create long vertical columns of curd in the cheese pot.

Now make horizontal cuts to create cubes of individual curds. You can use the curd knife to make these cuts by inserting it into the curd mass at a 45-degree angle and rotating it around the pot. Adjust the angle and rotate again. Continue this until most of the curd has been cut into pieces. Obviously you will not end up with perfect cubes of curd; the pieces will have irregular sizes. Don't worry—the cheese will be fine.

Cut curd grid.

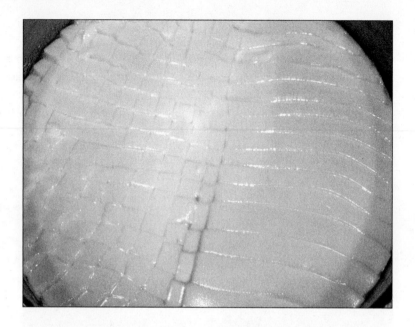

If you want more precision and control, you can make a custom curd cutter out of heavy (12-gauge) copper or steel electrical ground wire available from hardware stores. The total length should be a few inches longer than the depth plus half the diameter of your cheese pot. Hold the wire across the top of the pot to find the approximate center. Use the center reference to bend the wire at a 90-degree angle. The L-shaped cutter can now be inserted into the center of the curd mass and rotated to make cuts across the columns of curd. Make cuts parallel to the surface of the curd starting at the required size of curd pieces. If ½-inch curds are required, start ½ inch below the curd surface. Continue cutting parallel slices until you reach the bottom of the pot. Now you can use your spoon or curd knife and gently cut up any oversized pieces.

> **Whey Watch**
>
> It is more difficult to cut uniform pieces in a small batch of cheese. Do not risk overstirring the curd looking for large pieces. The cheese will be fine.

Once the curds are cut, the recipe will call for a rest period. During this time the curds are said to be "healing." Skipping this step will cause the curds to give up fat and protein to the whey, resulting in less cheese yield.

Curds after being cut.

Washing the Curd

The term "washed curd" refers to a treatment used to prepare curds for specific cheese styles. There are two ways of washing curds: warm and cold. The warm wash method is used at the beginning of the cooking process to quickly bring the curds up to the cooking temperature. This reduces the lactose content of the cheese and produces a firmer (lower moisture) curd. Using cold water to wash the curd is done after the cooking process and will result in a cheese with lower lactose but higher moisture content.

Cold washing can be done in the same manner as the warm water method but with cold water replacing some of the whey in order to lower the temperature. Colby cheese uses this method. Another method is to rinse the drained curds with cold running water. Cottage cheese is made this way. Both methods remove a small portion of both lactose and lactic acid.

Whey Watch

Do not confuse washed curd with washed rind. Washed curd cheeses have a portion of the whey replaced with water during curd processing to reduce acidity. Washed rind refers to the application of a "wash" of diluted salt brine (water, wine, beer, etc.) during the ripening stage of certain cheeses.

The warm washing process involves removing a portion of the whey from cut curds and replacing it with hot water. The hot water encourages more whey to be released and washes away some of the lactic acid, thus creating a "sweeter" and firmer cheese. Washed-curd cheeses are typically mild in flavor, store well, and are slower to age compared to many other cheeses. They are semi-firm in texture and may develop small eyes. Generally they have good melting properties. Gouda and Havarti are warm washed curd cheeses.

To warm wash the curds, you will need a pot of hot water ready for use. The cheese recipe will provide the temperatures, volumes, and timing for the warm washing process. The washing process starts with gently stirring the curds and whey. (Oversized curds can be cut to uniform size at this time.)

Cheese Bite

Only the original whey drained from washed-curd cheeses can be used to make ricotta cheese. Once the remaining whey is diluted with wash water, it is of no further use.

After the initial stirring, the curds are subjected to a process of settling, heating by hot water additions, and stirring. The timing and temperatures required are different for each recipe. Some cheeses will call for a portion of the whey to be removed and replaced with hot water. The number of reiterations will also depend on the cheese being made. Complete details for warm washing curds are given within each recipe.

The warm washing process is complete when curds pass the matting test. Take a handful of curds and gently squeeze them together. If they stick together but are easily separated using your fingers, they are ready to drain and press. If they do not mat, let them stay in the whey 5 minutes longer and then recheck.

Cooking Curds

After cutting the gel into the required-size pieces and allowing the curds to heal, they are ready for cooking. The temperature of the whey is increased according to the recipe. The cheese pot must be heated gradually, no more than 2°F every 5 minutes—the temperature is best controlled by placing the cheese pot into a hot water bath in a sink or large kettle. Adding hot water to the sink will increase the overall temperature and heat the cheese pot. Keep the bath water 10°F warmer than the target temperature for the curds. If the curd is heating too rapidly, simply take the pot out of the water for a while. Frequent gentle stirring will ensure even heating and prevent the curd pieces from matting together.

Draining

After reaching the proper firmness, the curds and whey are poured or ladled into a colander. The colander should rest in a sink or large container to permit collection of the whey. The curds are properly firmed when they have shrunk in size, are quite shiny, and are firm to the touch when lightly pressed between thumb and forefinger. When milk that has been pasteurized at higher temperatures is used, the curds will remain softer and may split open lightly when pressed between your fingers.

Cheddaring

In traditional cheddar cheese making, the process of cheddaring is used, which allows the drained curds to knit together and form a solid mass. The solid mass is then sliced into slabs and the slabs are stacked and flipped over a period of 2 hours. This process aids in the development of a firmer cheese. Complete step-by-step instructions for the cheddaring process are given in the Traditional Cheddar Cheese recipe in Chapter 9.

Cheese Bite

The origin of cheddar cheese dates back to the fifteenth century in Somerset, England. It gets its name from the Cheddar Caves where the cheese was first stored. Cheddar hasn't been stored there for years, but continues to be made in the West Country of Somerset.

Cheddar curd slabs after 2 hours.

Cheese Bite

USDA labeling standards state that when the word "cheese" is used alone in a manufactured product's name or ingredients statement, the cheese used must be cheddar.

Salting

After sufficient draining, the curds are salted right in the colander. The salt is sprinkled onto the curds and then gently mixed in. Salting will enhance the flavor of the cheese and aid in draining whey from the curd. The salt also assists in the final preservation of the cheese. Along with the salt, you may also add dried herbs such as sage or dried hot pepper flakes. Whole seeds like caraway can be a nice touch. Avoid fresh products, because the moisture will prevent the curds from knitting together.

Whey Watch

Herbs that you have picked and dried will contain unwanted bacteria and mold. They should be heated in the microwave to sanitize them just prior to adding to your cheese. This heat treatment will also release oils and other flavor compounds, further enhancing the cheese. Also remember that a little will go a long way.

Pressing

Making hard cheese requires the use of mechanically applied pressure to squeeze the curd in a process called knitting, as described in Chapter 3. Cheese curds have a thin membrane of fat on their surface. This prevents the curds from joining together on their own. As pressure is applied, the individual curds are squeezed, causing them to bulge. The fat membrane is forced open and the interior of the curd is exposed. When the casein of the exposed curds touch each other they bond together, creating a single block.

When the time comes to press your cheese, first line the mold you are using with a piece of sterile coarse cheesecloth, then place the curd into the lined mold. As you load curd into the mold, beware that some whey will begin draining. The whey that is pressed from the cheese must have a place to collect. Since there are holes in the bottom of the press, set the mold on a draining mat to keep it above the liquid. Please note that whey collected from your cheese press should be discarded.

The excess cloth is folded over the top of the curd. Avoid bunching up the cloth or the cheese will have an irregular surface, allowing for the formation of surface mold. The "follower" (discussed in Chapter 3), sometimes called a lid, is placed flat side down on top of the wrapped curds. Slight adjustments may be necessary to assure that the curd is level and the surface is flat. You should press down lightly on the follower to make sure that everything is stable.

The amount of pressure and time of pressing will depend on the type of cheese being made. Recipes will start the pressing with a few pounds of pressure and then increase the weight over time.

Cheese under pressure.

Whey Watch

You may be tempted to use the pressing method designed for one cheese style to make another. This most often occurs when making cheddar "style" cheese. The Traditional Cheddar Cheese recipe in Chapter 9 requires more weight for pressing due to the cheddaring process, and this cheese has low moisture content. Applying this same weight factor to the Farmhouse Cheddar recipe in Chapter 9 will result in a dry, brittle cheese.

Once the press is assembled, weight should be applied gently. Dropping weights onto the press will cause the curd to pack down, creating voids or pockets of whey inside the cheese. Center the weights carefully on the follower. Off-center weights may tilt and bind the follower against the wall of the mold.

Each cheese recipe will provide you with a pressing schedule. This is a sequence of weights and time periods between turnings. Your cheese must be turned on the specified schedule. This provides for the even pressing and equal distribution of the remaining moisture into the cheese. To turn the cheese, carefully lift off the weights, then lift the press by slipping one hand under the basket and placing the other on top. Turn the entire assembly over and then remove the mold. This will leave the cheese sitting on top of the follower. Carefully lift the cheese, unwrap it, turn it over, rewrap, and place it back into the mold. Place the follower on top, add the weights, and continue the pressing process.

Aging and Storing

In this step, the cheese is prepared for both safekeeping and eating. The exact procedures and environmental conditions will be determined by the style of cheese you are making. In general, you need to provide stable temperature and humidity suited to the cheeses' requirements.

Air Drying

After draining and/or pressing, the cheese may require time for its surface to dry. Remove the cheese from the cheesecloth wrap and place it on a clean drying mat to air dry. Protect the cheese from pests by covering it loosely with clean cheesecloth. Turn the cheese twice each day until the surface is dry.

> **Whey Watch**
>
> Cheese that is dried too quickly will show cracks in the surface. Even cracks that are barely visible can become a hiding place for unwanted bacteria that then have the potential of being sealed in under the wax.

The air flow must not be drafty but there should be some ventilation provided. It can take 1 to 3 days for a cheese to dry depending on humidity levels. It is possible for a cheese to become overly dry within a short period of time in areas where the humidity is low, thus causing cracks in the rind.

Pressed cheese left to dry.

Rind Development

As the cheese cures, the rind will begin to develop. This rind will have many forms depending on the cheese being made. Bloomy and smear rind development require the strict environmental controls provided by a cheese cave as described in Chapter 3. Without these controls, the rind will be over- or underdeveloped, resulting in spoiled cheese.

Some cheese styles require special surface treatments for their rind development, such as the application of salt, washes, or microflora. Many mold-ripened cheeses receive a light spray of diluted mold culture before being placed in the aging container. The mold will produce the bloomy rind found on cheeses like Brie and Camembert. The spray method works well for larger-scale cheese production. However, for the home cheesemaker it is more practical to inoculate the milk as part of the acidification step. The inoculation method works because mold growth requires oxygen, so the only place you will see visible bloom is on the surface of the cheese.

Washed-rind cheeses can utilize a variety of washes while ripening. Water, salt brine, beer, or wine may be used in making Muenster, brick, or Limburger cheeses. While in the aging container the cheese is wiped or "washed" with one of these solutions in order to spread or "smear" the inoculated bacteria over the entire surface. This will control the mold growth on the rind. The process of rind washing is done on a regular schedule (such as every other day) until the desired result is achieved.

Waxing and Wrapping

Waxing is the traditional method of sealing a cheese for aging. Special cheese wax gives the best results. The wax must be melted in a double boiler to reduce the danger of fire. A 1 quart reusable food storage container with a snap-on lid or a disposable foil pan is perfect for melting and storing cheese wax. The wax should be in a completely liquid state prior to application on the cheese.

The size and shape of your wax container will determine the size of the cheese you can manage, and the size of the waxed cheese will affect the aging process. The cheese wheels produced by the recommended Tomme press (see Chapter 3) can be managed pretty well. You may elect to cut the wheels in half or quarters prior to waxing; however, making the cheese smaller is not recommended.

You will need a nonstick surface to cool the hot waxed cheese. Prepare your work area by placing a sheet of waxed paper or parchment paper on the counter next to your stove. Place the wax container into a larger pan of water and heat the water to a simmer. When the wax is melted, turn the heat down.

Whey Watch

Wax is extremely flammable. Never melt wax over direct heat and never use a microwave oven to melt wax. Also keep molten wax away from small children!

Dipping is the best way to coat the cheese in wax.

The best way to coat the cheese in wax is to dip it directly into the liquid wax. Hold one edge of the cheese and dip the other edge into the melted wax. Hold it there for 2 seconds. Leaving the cheese in the hot wax for too long will cause the surface of the cheese to soften. Lift the cheese and allow the wax to harden. This will only take about 30 seconds. Lay the cheese down on a nonstick surface and allow the wax to cool. Pick up the cheese by the waxed side and dip the other side. Repeat the cooling process.

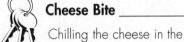

Cheese Bite

Chilling the cheese in the freezer for a few minutes before waxing and in between coats will aid in the adhesion of the wax.

Depending on the temperature of the wax, it may adhere to the cheese in a thick or thin coat. With practice you will learn to adjust the temperature to get a smooth, even coating. It may be necessary to dip the cheese multiple times.

Inspect the cheese for bubbles or blisters in the wax. Use a small, natural boar bristle paintbrush or pastry brush to touch up any holes or exposed areas. These brushes are available at kitchen supply shops and craft and hardware stores. Note that once the brush is used for waxing, it will only be suited for waxing.

Touch up the wax with a brush.

On a small piece of paper, write down the type of cheese, the date, and any other useful information. Place the note on the cheese and use the brush to lightly paint over it. You will be able to read the message through the wax. This will provide a record of the type of cheese and when it was produced. Place the finished wheel on the waxed paper and allow it to cool completely.

An alternative to waxing is to use a food storage vacuum system to seal your cheese for storage. We have had excellent results with this method and enjoy the ease with which you can sample a cheese and then reseal it. You must use the air-proof packaging recommended by the system's manufacturer.

Once waxed, the cheese should be aged at a temperature between 40°F and 60°F. Turn the cheese over daily for the first 2 weeks or moisture will accumulate on the bottom. The cheese must be turned at least once a week. If you are using raw milk (unpasteurized), age the cheese for at least 60 days at a temperature close to 50°F.

The Cheesemaker's Worksheet

It is easy to become confused during the preparation of a cheese batch, and interruptions are inevitable. Since you will want a record of the process for each batch you make, make a working copy of the recipe and use it to record notes as you make the cheese. See the Cheesemaker's Worksheet in Appendix C for an example. This written record will be very useful as you troubleshoot your cheese-making process and work to improve and refine the quality of your cheeses.

The Least You Need to Know

- A specific organized sequence of steps is necessary for each type of cheese you're making.

- Rennet enables the coagulation of the milk protein into a solid curd and facilitates gel formation.

- Curds must rest after they have been cut.

- Rind aids in the aging process, and its development can occur naturally or be applied using wax.

Chapter 8

Processed-Curd Cheeses

In This Chapter

♦ Applying curd cutting and cooking techniques with cottage cheese

♦ How to make hoop cheese

♦ Using lipase powder in queso fresco

The recipes in this chapter provide experience manipulating curds. Apply the knowledge and skills you've gained thus far to make delicious cottage cheese, semi-soft hoop cheese, and the Mexican-style cheese queso fresco.

Large-Curd Cottage Cheese

This is an old-fashioned large-curd cottage cheese with a clean acid flavor. Keep this cheese under refrigeration in an airtight container for up to a week.

Yield: *1½ pounds*
Prep time: 3 hours
Rest time: 1 hour

Ingredients:

1 gallon whole milk

½ tsp. prepared calcium chloride

¼ tsp. mesophilic culture

½ prepared rennet tablet

¼ tsp. cheese salt

Equipment:

Cheese pot

Thermometer

Curd knife

Slotted spoon

Measuring spoons

Colander or strainer

1 yard fine cheesecloth

1. Place milk into the cheese pot and gently heat to 86°F.

2. Add calcium chloride to milk and stir gently for 30 seconds. Sprinkle culture over milk surface and let rehydrate for 1 or 2 minutes. Gently and thoroughly stir culture into milk. Let milk ripen with the cover on at 86°F for 30 minutes.

Tasty Chatter

Making this delicious Old World–style cottage cheese requires a number of curd-processing techniques. It is the perfect way for you to experience gel development and testing for a clean break. Cottage cheese is a stirred curd cheese. The curds must be cut into uniform pieces, cooked and stirred, and then cold washed. The process results in a mild, slightly dry cottage cheese.

3. Stir rennet gently into the milk. Cover and allow milk to rest undisturbed for 30 to 45 minutes at 86°F, or calculate the flocculation time as described in Chapter 7. Test gel for a clean break.

4. When gel displays a clean break, cut curds into ½-inch slices with a curd knife. Turn the pot 90 degrees and repeat. The top of the gel should look like a crossword puzzle.

5. Continue using the curd knife to gently break curds into approximate ½-inch cubes. Be very gentle and do not make the pieces too small. Avoid mashing curds together.

6. Slowly heat curds, in a double boiler or kitchen sink full of water, to 115°F by increasing curd temperature 2°F every 5 minutes until the target temperature is reached. Curds will shrink as the heat forces whey out. The entire cooking process can take from 1 to 1½ hours.

7. Line a colander with fine cheesecloth. Pour curds and whey into the colander and allow to drain for 5 minutes.

8. Take the bag of curds and rinse in cool water. This removes additional whey, reduces the acidity of the cheese, and prevents curds from matting together. Hang curds to drain for 1 hour.

9. Remove cheese from the cheesecloth and place in a bowl. Break up curd mass into smaller pieces with your hands, but do so gently. The size of the finished curds is up to you. Finish by tossing in salt.

Cheese Bite

For a creamier version of cottage cheese, simply add a little fresh milk or cream before storing the finished cheese.

Cheese Blintzes

These tender crepes are filled with a creamy, spice-infused cheese mixture complemented by sour cream and sweet fruit toppings.

Yield: *4 servings of 3 blintzes*

Prep time: 1 hour
Cook time: 15 minutes

Ingredients:

1 cup milk

3 eggs

1 tsp. salt

2 TB. melted butter

¾ cup sifted flour

2 cups cottage cheese

1 egg yolk

2 TB. sugar

½ tsp. vanilla

¼ tsp. ground cinnamon

Pinch ground nutmeg

1. Place milk, eggs, ½ teaspoon salt, butter, and flour in a blender and mix until smooth. Pour into a bowl and let sit for 30 minutes. In the meantime, prepare filling.

2. Place cottage cheese, egg yolk, ½ tsp. salt, sugar, vanilla, cinnamon, and nutmeg in a blender. Mix until combined. If filling is too runny, thicken by adding 1 tablespoon flour.

3. Heat a small skillet or crepe pan and coat with butter. Use 2 tablespoons crepe batter for each blintz. Pour batter into the pan and tilt to coat evenly. Brown bottom side then flip crepe over, briefly warming uncooked side. Stack finished crepes between paper towels until all are cooked.

4. Place 1 heaping tablespoon filling on each crepe. Fold sides in and roll up like a jelly roll. Place seam-side down in a buttered baking dish and bake at 425°F for 10 to 15 minutes or until browned on top and heated through.

5. Serve with sour cream and your favorite fruit topping or apple butter.

Hoop or Farmer's Cheese

Hoop cheese is a semi-soft fresh cheese similar in flavor to cottage cheese but in a pressed form. Its other name, farmer's cheese, comes from its origin as a quick rustic cheese made by farmers for their own consumption. The flavor is like tangy cottage cheese.

Ingredients:

3 gallons whole milk

1½ tsp. prepared calcium chloride solution

¼ tsp. mesophilic culture

½ prepared rennet tablet

Equipment:

Cheese pot

Thermometer

Curd knife

Slotted spoon

Measuring spoons

Colander or strainer

Coarse cheesecloth

#10 clean steel can (top and bottom removed)

Yield: *3 to 3¼ pounds*
Prep time: 2½ hours
Rest time: 12 hours

1. Combine milk and calcium chloride in a cheese pot. Slowly heat mixture to 90°F. Stir to prevent milk from scorching.

2. Turn off heat and sprinkle culture onto milk surface. Allow culture to rehydrate for 2 or 3 minutes before stirring into milk. Cover the pot and allow milk to acidify at 90°F for 45 minutes.

Cheese Bite _____

A #10 steel can is the large, institutional-size container of canned goods like tomato sauce or vegetables. One can holds about 1 gallon of liquid.

3. Add rennet and stir gently into 90°F milk, using an up-and-down motion. Let milk set covered for 30 to 40 minutes or until curds show a clean break.

Dressed hoop in sink.

4. Use a curd knife to cut curds into ½-inch cubes. Use a water bath to heat curds and whey to 100°F, increasing the temperature no faster than 2°F every 5 minutes. It should

take 30 minutes to reach 100°F. This is best done by maintaining the bath water at 100°F to 110°F. Stir frequently but gently to prevent curds from matting.

5. Place a large colander in the sink. Pour curds and whey into the colander and allow to drain. Gently sift through curds with clean hands to facilitate draining. This will unblock the draining holes and keep curds from matting together.

Hoop loaded with curd.

6. Place curds into a cloth-lined hoop. Press with 4 to 5 pounds of weight for 15 minutes.

7. Remove the weight and follower. Turn the entire press end over end with cheese inside. You may have to firmly tap the can down on the draining board to release cheese, as a slight vacuum is created. Press cheese with 8 to 10 pounds of pressure for 12 hours. It is not unusual for the saucer to become bound up in the hoop. Check on it once or twice and make adjustments as needed.

Hoop cheese being pressed.

8. Remove cheese from the press and unwrap the cloth. Cheese is ready to eat immediately or may be wrapped and stored in the refrigerator for up to 1 week.

Finished hoop cheese.

Using Lipase Powder

The next recipe introduces a new ingredient, lipase. Lipase is an enzyme found in raw milk and is a major contributor to the final character of raw milk cheeses. The enzyme splits milkfat molecules into fatty acids that create distinctive flavors referred to as *picante*. The breakdown of fat takes place during aging, and the flavors permeate the finished cheese. The longer the aging period, the stronger the picante flavor. It is possible to overage a lipase cheese such that it creates an undesirable or boring flavor profile. Provolone, which is considered inferior due to overripening or misapplication of lipase, is used for cooking or as a topping for pizza.

def•i•ni•tion

The word **picante** is used in cheese making to describe the characteristic sharp flavor of cheese styles like provolone and parmesan. This flavor develops naturally in raw milk cheeses.

Unfortunately, pasteurization deactivates lipase. For this reason, lipase is available in powdered form for use in cheese making. The enzyme is added to pasteurized cheese milk at the beginning of the cheese-making process and is carried through to the curds during coagulation. Mild lipase powder is considered a must-have ingredient for the production of mild provolone and other Italian-style cheeses. Without lipase, these cheeses will never develop their full flavor.

Lipase powder must be dissolved in distilled water just prior to being added to milk. The amount of powder used will depend on the cheese style and volume of cheese milk. Excessive application of lipase can interfere with curd formation. Combine the required amount of powder with 2 tablespoons of distilled water and allow it to rest for 10 minutes. This helps to integrate the lipase with the milk without excessive stirring.

Once you have prepared a recipe using lipase powder, you may want to reduce the amount used to suit your taste. You should not increase the amount. The picante flavor does not come from the powder but rather from what the enzyme does to the milkfat. To increase the intensity of the flavor, the cheese must be aged for a longer period of time.

Whey Watch

Lipase powder may not be suitable for some vegetarian diets. Unfortunately, there is no substitute. Lipase can be omitted from any recipe, but the cheese will lack the expected flavor.

Queso Fresco

Queso fresco means "fresh cheese" in Spanish. It is a moist cheese that easily crumbles onto Mexican-style dishes, making it a Central American staple. When heated, the cheese becomes creamy.

Yield: *3 to 3½ pounds*
Prep time: 3 hours
Rest time: 8 hours + optional 2 days aging

Ingredients:

3 gallons whole milk

1½ tsp. liquid calcium chloride

¼ tsp. mesophilic culture

¼ tsp. mild lipase powder

½ prepared rennet tablet

3 TB. cheese salt

Equipment:

Cheese pot

Thermometer

Curd knife

Slotted spoon

Measuring spoons

Colander or strainer

1 yard coarse cheesecloth

Tomme cheese press with 3 10-lb. weights

1. Combine milk and calcium chloride in a cheese pot. Slowly heat mixture to 90°F, stirring to prevent milk from scorching.

2. Sprinkle culture over milk surface and let rehydrate for 1 or 2 minutes. Gently and thoroughly stir culture into milk. Stir in lipase powder. Cover and hold at 90°F for 1 hour.

3. Add rennet and stir in gently using an up-and-down motion. Hold at 90°F for 1 hour.

4. Cut curd mass into ¼-inch cubes and let rest for 10 minutes. Stir curds gently. Heat curds slowly to 99°F over a 20-minute period, stirring occasionally. Let curds rest for 5 minutes.

5. Tip the pot to drain whey over a large colander, in order to catch curds. Add salt and mix gently but thoroughly with your hands. Set the pot of salted curds in a water bath of 100°F for 20 minutes.

6. Place curds into a cheesecloth-lined cheese press mold. Follow instructions for pressing (see Chapter 7) and press with a 10-pound weight for 10 minutes. Turn cheese over, rewrap, and press with 20 pounds for 1 hour. Turn, rewrap,

> **Tasty Chatter**
>
> The Queso Fresco recipe combines a new ingredient (lipase powder) with the use of the Tomme cheese press. The detailed instructions for using the press are provided in Chapter 7, while the specific weights and pressing times are provided in the recipe. Using the proper press will give you the best results.

and press with 30 pounds for 6 hours. Cheese may be eaten now but may benefit from a 2-day aging period in the refrigerator. Queso fresco will keep for up to 2 weeks when wrapped and refrigerated.

Finished queso fresco.

Jalapeño Corn Muffins with Queso Fresco Crumbles

The creaminess of the melted fresh cheese gives your taste buds relief from the spicy peppers. Both the cheese and peppers are complimented by the tangy buttermilk and sweet corn.

Ingredients:

1 cup all-purpose flour

1 cup yellow cornmeal

2 tsp. baking powder

½ tsp. baking soda

½ tsp. salt

Pinch cayenne pepper

½ cup crumbled queso fresco

1 cup buttermilk

¼ cup vegetable oil

2 large eggs, lightly beaten

1 to 2 TB. seeded and minced jalapeños

3 TB. sugar

Yield: *12 muffins*	
Prep time: 15 minutes	
Cook time: 15 minutes	

1. Preheat the oven to 375°F. Lightly grease 12 regular-size muffin tin cups or line with paper liners.

2. In a large bowl, mix together flour, cornmeal, baking powder, baking soda, salt, and cayenne pepper. Then stir cheese crumbles into dry mixture.

3. In a second bowl, whisk together buttermilk, oil, eggs, jalapeños, and sugar. Add liquid mixture to dry mixture and stir just until moistened.

4. Spoon batter into prepared muffin tins, filling them only ¾ full.

5. Bake muffins until golden and a toothpick inserted into the center comes out clean, approximately 12 to 15 minutes.

6. Transfer to a wire rack to cool. Serve warm.

Take Stock of Your Skills

The preceding recipes have taught you how to develop and manipulate cheese curds using standardized techniques, and how to combine your homemade cheese into other recipes for even more tasty results. You now have firsthand experience with the processes used, and you should have the ability to recognize the transformation stages displayed by the milk as it becomes cheese. It is best that you make sure you are very comfortable with your skills to this point before moving on to the next chapter. Do not hesitate to make the cheeses again to hone your cheese-making skills.

The Least You Need to Know

- Making cottage cheese is an exercise in testing the development of the gel.

- Lipase powder is an enzyme that enables the flavor development known as picante.

- Farmer's cheese is made using a cheese hoop that can be made out of a large #10 steel can.

- Queso fresco is fresh cheese that uses lipase powder in its processing.

Chapter 9

Hard Cheese Recipes

In This Chapter

- Working with cheddar, Monterey Jack, and Colby recipes
- Applying the cheddaring process
- Squeaky cheese curd
- Making traditional cheddar

The recipes in this chapter are in order of the skills required. The ingredients may look the same, but there is something unique to each recipe that contributes to the characteristics of the final product. You should start with the Farmhouse Cheddar recipe and continue through to the Traditional Cheddar Cheese recipe. If you are inclined to skip a cheese, please take the time to read through the recipe until you are confident of the steps that make it unique. Remember that uniqueness comes from both ingredients and process.

A key difference in the recipes is the time it will take for the cheese to be ready to consume. The "youngest cheeses" appear first in the chapter, providing you the opportunity to enjoy and share your creations quickly. You will also find that as you move deeper into the chapter, the number of steps required to make the cheese will increase along with the time it takes to complete them.

All of the recipes call for 3 or 4 gallons of milk. This amount of milk is necessary to produce enough curd to make the Tomme cheese press work effectively. Your yields will be 3 to 3½ pounds of cheese depending on the recipe size. You will need a minimum cheese pot size of 16 quarts (4 gallons) to produce these recipes and a 20-quart pot for the Traditional Cheddar Cheese recipe.

Farmhouse Cheddar

Farmhouse cheddar is a hard cheese made using a few shortcuts to produce a cheese that's rustic in appearance but similar in flavor to cheddar. It's a good choice for the first-time hard cheese-maker since it won't take as much time as traditional cheddar.

> **Yield:** *3 to 3¼ pounds*
>
> **Prep time:** 3½ hours
>
> **Rest time:** 3 days to 3 months

Ingredients:

3 gallons whole milk

1 pint heavy cream

1½ tsp. prepared liquid calcium chloride

¼ tsp. mesophilic culture

½ prepared rennet tablet

4 TB. flaked salt

½ cup distilled water

Equipment:

Cheese pot

Slotted spoon

Curd knife

Colander or strainer

Coarse cheesecloth

Tomme press with weights

Bamboo drying mat

Cheese wax (optional)

> **Tasty Chatter**
>
> Farmhouse cheddar is ready to eat as soon as it is made. It will also improve in flavor with a short aging period.

1. Combine milk, cream, and calcium chloride in a cheese pot or double boiler. Gently heat mixture to 90°F. Stir with an easy push-pull action to prevent milk from scorching.

2. Turn off heat and sprinkle culture onto milk surface. Allow culture to rehydrate for 3 minutes before stirring into milk. Cover the pot and allow milk to rest at 90°F for 45 minutes.

3. Note the time and add rennet by mixing into milk with an up-and-down motion for about 1 minute. Monitor gel development with the method described in Chapter 7, using the rate factor of 3. It should be between 30 and 40 minutes. After the set time has elapsed, check curds for a clean break.

4. Use a curd knife to cut gel into ½-inch cubes. Allow curds to heal for 5 minutes.

5. Indirectly heat curds to 100°F by increasing the temperature no faster than 2°F every 5 minutes. It should take 30 minutes to reach 100°F. This is best achieved in a double boiler on the stove top or in a sink full of 100°F to 110°F water. Stir frequently but gently to prevent matting.

6. Hold curds and whey at 100°F for 1 hour, stirring every 5 minutes to keep curds from matting together. Adjust the temperature of your double boiler or sink water as needed to maintain this temperature.

7. Place a large colander in the sink. (Note that no cheesecloth is used here.) Carefully pour curds and whey into the colander and allow to drain. Gently sift through curds with clean hands to facilitate draining. This will unblock the draining holes and keep curds from matting. Once whey has drained, sprinkle 1 tablespoon salt over curds and gently mix it in using your hands. Wait 1 minute and repeat with 1 tablespoon salt. Wait 1 minute and repeat with 1 tablespoon salt.

8. Place curds into a cloth-lined press basket as described in Chapter 7. Press with 4 to 5 pounds of weight for 15 minutes.

9. Remove cheese from the press and take it out of the cheesecloth. Place the cheesecloth back in the mold and return cheese to the mold upside down. This time, press the cheese with 8 to 10 pounds of pressure for 12 hours.

10. Remove cheese from the press as before and unwrap the cloth. Prepare brine solution with 1 tablespoon salt in distilled water. Using a corner of the cheesecloth, lightly apply saltwater wash to cheese. Paint the solution on; do not rub it in.

11. Place cheese on a bamboo mat to air dry for 1 to 3 days. Cheese must be turned over twice a day. Cheese is ready to eat when yellowish rind (similar to the color of butter) starts to develop and cheese is dry to the touch. Left unwaxed, cheese should be refrigerated and consumed within 2 weeks.

12. You can age cheese for up to 3 months by sealing it in cheese wax or by vacuum packing as described in Chapter 7. Cheese will benefit from storage in a constant temperature between 45°F and 60°F. Cheese will mature more quickly at the warmer end of the range.

≈⌐

Turkey Farmhouse Rollups

The slight sharpness of farmhouse cheddar will complement the sweet smokiness of the turkey. The colorful veggies add crunch and make the rolls look as good as they taste.

Yield: *4 rollups*
Prep time: 20 minutes

Ingredients:

3 oz. Neufchâtel or light cream cheese

1 avocado, peeled and pitted

1 TB. lemon juice

⅛ tsp. garlic powder

¼ tsp. salt

4 large flour tortillas

½ lb. (8 slices) deli-sliced smoked turkey

½ package (3 oz.) fresh baby spinach leaves

½ cup shredded carrots

2 plum tomatoes, seeded and chopped

½ cup (4 oz.) farmhouse cheddar, crumbled

1. Mix Neufchâtel, avocado, lemon juice, garlic powder, and salt until smooth.

2. Spread each tortilla with 2 tablespoons Neufchâtel and avocado mixture. Arrange 2 turkey slices atop each, then divide spinach, carrots, tomatoes, and cheddar evenly over turkey.

3. Roll up each filled tortilla tightly and secure with toothpicks at both ends. Cut each in half diagonally and serve.

Monterey Jack

Monterey Jack or Jack cheese is a soft, white cheese with a slight tang. It is ready to eat after a month of aging. A more acidic tang will develop with longer aging.

Ingredients:

3 gallons whole milk

1 pint heavy cream (optional)

1½ tsp. prepared calcium chloride solution

¼ tsp. mesophilic culture

½ prepared rennet tablet

4 TB. flaked salt

½ cup water

Equipment:

Cheese pot

Thermometer

Curd knife

Slotted spoon

Measuring spoons

Colander or strainer

Coarse cheesecloth

Tomme press with weights

Bamboo drying mat

Cheese wax

Yield: *3 to 3¼ pounds*
Prep time: 3½ hours
Rest time: 1 to 4 months

1. Combine milk, cream (if using), and calcium chloride in a cheese pot within a double boiler. Heat milk to 88°F.

2. Turn off heat and sprinkle culture onto milk surface. Allow culture to rehydrate for 3 minutes before stirring in. Allow milk to ripen for 45 minutes.

3. Note the time then add rennet and stir gently into milk, using an up-and-down motion. Let milk set, covered, at 88°F for 30 to 40 minutes or until curds show a clean break. You may use the gel development test described in Chapter 7 to more closely estimate the setting time, using the rate factor of 3. After the set time has elapsed, check curds for a clean break.

4. Once you see a clean break, use a curd knife to cut gel into ½-inch cubes. Let curds heal for 5 minutes.

5. Slowly heat the water in the double boiler to 100°F. This will indirectly heat curds to 100°F by increasing the temperature no faster than 2°F every 5 minutes. It should take

Tasty Chatter

Monterey Jack, or Jack cheese, is believed to have been created by David Jacks near Monterey, California, in the 1890s. Authentic California Jack cheese has a tiny eye structure throughout, while Jack cheese made elsewhere has no eye structure.

30 minutes. Stir gently but frequently to keep curds from matting together. Maintain curds at 100°F for an additional 30 minutes, stirring every several minutes to keep curds from matting. Allow curds to settle for 5 minutes.

6. Pour or ladle off whey down to the curds and maintain a temperature of 100°F. Allow curds to set for 30 minutes, stirring every 5 minutes to prevent matting.

7. Place a large colander in the sink. Pour curds and whey into the colander and allow whey to drain. To facilitate draining, gently sift through curds with clean hands. Unblock the draining holes as necessary and keep curds from matting. Once whey has drained, sprinkle 1 tablespoon salt over curds and gently mix in using your hands. Wait 1 minute and repeat with 1 tablespoon salt. Wait 1 minute and repeat with another tablespoon salt.

8. Follow directions in Chapter 7 for using the Tomme cheese press. Press cheese with 4 to 5 pounds of weight for 15 minutes. Turn cheese as described and press for 12 hours with 8 to 10 pounds of weight.

9. Remove cheese from the press as before and unwrap the cloth. Mix 1 tablespoon salt with water. Using a corner of the cheesecloth, lightly apply saltwater wash to cheese.

10. Place salted cheese on a bamboo mat to air dry for 1 to 3 days. Cover with a clean cheesecloth. Turn cheese over twice each day. When it starts to form a yellowish rind and is dry to the touch, it is ready to wax for storage.

11. Wax cheese and store for aging at 40°F to 60°F (55°F is ideal) for 1 to 4 months. Turn the cheese over daily for the first month and several times a week thereafter.

Oily or wet ingredients should not be used. These will prevent the curds from knitting in the cheese press. You should also avoid using ingredients that are prone to spoilage, may contain bacteria, or have flavors which weaken and become bitter over time.

Cheese Bite

Adding hot peppers to a cheese is one of the most popular recipe variations. Monterey Jack has a flavor profile and texture that is perfect for "jacking up" the heat. Any variety of crushed pepper flakes will work. If you prefer, finely minced pickled jalapeños are a nice addition.

Whey Watch

Fresh minced peppers can also be used provided they are blanched in boiling water for 1 minute prior to putting them into the cheese.

Cheese Bite _____

Dairy products, including cheese, are the best prescription for overly spicy foods. The heat in hot chilies comes from a chemical called capsaicin. Capsaicin is not soluble in water, so when it gets on your tongue it stays there. Capsaicin will, however, bond with milk casein (protein) and be carried away.

Colby Cheese

Colby's flavor is similar to but milder than cheddar and has a softer texture. Colby cheese can be eaten right after it is made or aged for 2 to 3 months.

Ingredients:

3 gallons whole milk

6 to 12 drops annatto cheese colorant (optional)

1½ tsp. prepared calcium chloride solution

¼ tsp. mesophilic culture

½ prepared rennet tablet

4 TB. flaked salt

½ cup water

Equipment:

Cheese pot

Thermometer

Curd knife

Slotted spoon

Measuring spoons

Colander or strainer

Coarse cheesecloth

Tomme press with weights

Bamboo drying mat

Cheese wax

Yield: _3 to 3¼ pounds_	
Prep time: 3½ hours	
Rest time: 14 hours to 3 months	

1. Combine milk, annatto (if using), and calcium chloride in a cheese pot. Slowly heat mixture to 86°F. Stir to prevent milk from scorching.

2. Turn off heat and sprinkle culture onto milk surface. Allow culture to rehydrate for 2 or 3 minutes before stirring in. Cover the pot and allow to acidify at 86°F for 1 hour.

3. Add rennet and stir gently into milk, using an up-and-down motion. Let milk set, covered, at 86°F for 30 to 40 minutes

or until curd shows a clean break. You may elect to use the gel development test described in Chapter 7 to more closely estimate the setting time.

Tasty Chatter
Colby was invented in Colby, Wisconsin, in the late nineteenth or early twentieth century. The "Colby process" used to make the cheese is similar to that used to make traditional cheddar but omits the actual cheddaring step and a procedure in which the curds are "washed" with cool water to increase their moisture content.

4. When gel demonstrates a clean break, cut curds into ⅜-inch cubes. Stir gently, then let curds heal for 5 minutes.

Cheese Bite _____

Colby cheese gets its distinctive color from the addition of annatto coloring. You may choose to add annatto coloring to give your cheese the traditional orange appearance. Annatto, like rennet, will lose its potency over time and with exposure to light. Start by adding 2 to 3 drops per gallon of milk. Mix color in until evenly dispersed.

5. Using a water bath, slowly stir and heat curds and whey to 102°F by increasing the temperature no faster than 2°F every 5 minutes. This should take about 30 minutes. Hold the temperature at 102°F for 30 more minutes, gently stirring every 5 minutes so that curds do not mat.

6. Cover the pot and allow curds to settle for 5 minutes.

7. Pour off whey until level with curd mass. Stir in cold tap water until the cheese pot temperature is 80°F. Hold at 80°F for 15 minutes, gently stirring to keep curds from matting. The temperature of the cheese pot during this step will determine moisture content of finished cheese. A slightly higher temperature will produce a drier cheese. Lowering the temperature a few degrees will make a moister cheese.

8. Place a large colander in the sink and pour curds and whey into the colander, allowing whey to drain. Gently sift through curds with clean hands to facilitate draining. This will unblock the draining holes and keep curds from matting together. Once whey has drained, sprinkle 1 tablespoon salt over curds and gently mix in using your hands. Wait 1 minute and repeat with 1 tablespoon salt. Wait 1 minute and repeat with another tablespoon salt.

9. Prepare coarse cheesecloth for use in your cheese press. Follow the instructions given in Chapter 7 using 20 pounds of weight for 20 minutes. Turn cheese over and press again with 30 pounds for 20 minutes. Turn cheese a third time and press with 50 pounds for 12 hours.

Cheese Bite

If you have the capacity to make two cheese recipes at one time, you can prepare the classic combination of Monterey Jack and Yellow Colby. Both recipes are prepared independently of each other up to the point of pressing. The curds are mixed together just before they are placed into the press. The finished cheese will show a distinctive yellow-and-white mottling and have the flavor of both cheeses.

10. Remove cheese from the press and remove the cheesecloth. Prepare saltwater wash by mixing 1 tablespoon salt with water. Using a corner of the cheesecloth, lightly apply saltwater wash to cheese. Paint solution on; do not rub it in. Place cheese on a bamboo mat to air dry for 1 to 3 days, turning over twice each day. When it starts to form a yellowish rind and is dry to the touch, it is ready to wax for aging.

11. Wax cheese as described in Chapter 7. Store for aging at 40°F to 60°F (55°F is ideal) for 2 to 3 months. Turn cheese over daily for the first month and several times a week thereafter.

Acorn Squash Stuffed with Sausage and Colby

In this recipe, the mild Colby cheese creates a bridge between the sweet squash and savory sausage.

Yield: *4 servings of ½ squash*
Prep time: 15 minutes
Cook time: 45 minutes

Ingredients:

2 acorn squash, cut in half lengthwise

½ lb. bulk pork sausage

1 medium onion, diced in quarters

1 medium apple, peeled, cored, and diced in quarters

2 tsp. fresh sage or ½ tsp. dried sage

¼ tsp. ground black pepper

½ cup fresh breadcrumbs

1½ cups (6 oz.) shredded Colby cheese

1. Preheat the oven to 375°F. Halve and seed squash; place halves cut sides down in a shallow baking pan. Fill the pan with ½ inch water and cover with foil. Bake for 30 to 40 minutes or until squash is tender when pierced. Allow to cool slightly.

2. Meanwhile, crumble sausage in a large skillet and cook over medium heat until no longer pink. Pour off fat. Add onion, apple, sage, and black pepper to sausage and cook over medium-low heat. Stir occasionally until softened, approximately 10 to 15 minutes.

3. Add breadcrumbs and mix to combine. Continue cooking until most of the moisture has evaporated, about 5 minutes. Remove from heat.

4. Add 1 cup Colby and stir in.

5. Discard water from the baking pan of squash. Turn squash right-side up and fill cavities with sausage and cheese mixture, dividing evenly. Sprinkle tops with remaining Colby and place in the oven for 5 minutes or until cheese has melted. Serve hot.

Squeaky Cheese Curds

Everyone in Wisconsin and anyone who lives near a cheese factory knows the joy of freshly made, squeaky cheese curds. These salty little cheddar-style gems are a great snack food.

Ingredients:

1 gallon whole milk (nonhomogenized for best "squeak")

½ tsp. calcium chloride solution

¼ tsp. mesophilic culture

½ prepared rennet tablet

2 tsp. flaked salt

Equipment:

Cheese pot

Slotted spoon

Colander or strainer

Curd knife

Cutting board

Yield: *1 to 1½ pounds*	
Prep Time: 4 hours	

1. Combine milk and calcium chloride in the cheese pot. Heat milk to 86°F.

2. Sprinkle culture onto milk surface and let rehydrate for 2 minutes. Gently mix culture into milk using an up-and-down motion. Cover pot and allow milk to ripen for 45 minutes.

3. Add rennet and gently mix using an up-and-down motion. Cover pot and allow milk to set for 30 to 45 minutes. Check gel for a clean break.

Tasty Chatter

Making squeaky curds will demonstrate the process of cheddaring described in Chapter 7. This recipe prepares you for making traditional cheddar cheese.

Squeaky cheese has the odd texture character of being firm yet chewy. The name comes from the sound made when the curd pieces rub against your teeth while being eaten. The best squeak comes on the day the cheese is made, and it will fade with time. Squeaky cheese is considered a fresh cheese because there is no drying or aging process. For this reason it doesn't travel well, so it is not available everywhere. Fortunately, you can make your own.

Cheese Bite

The Finns have a tradition of eating squeaky cheese called leipäjuusto or juusto. This cheese is prepared fresh then flattened onto a cookie sheet and broiled until golden on both sides.

def•i•ni•tion

Milling is the process of cutting up large cheese curds into uniform pieces. When the word *mill* is used, instead of "cut" or "break up," the implication is that the sizing and shape must be more precise.

4. When gel shows a clean break, cut into ½-inch cubes. Allow curds to heal for 5 minutes.

5. Gently begin stirring curds, cutting any larger pieces into smaller ones. Apply heat to slowly bring the temperature to 100°F, gently stirring the whole time. This should take 30 minutes. Avoid heating too quickly. If the temperature rises too fast, remove the cheese pot from heat for a few minutes. Resume gently heating and stirring.

6. After reaching 100°F, hold this temperature for another 30 minutes. Stir occasionally (every 5 minutes) to keep curds from matting. Placing the pot into a water bath at 100°F will help maintain the temperature.

7. After 30 minutes, check curds for matting. If they mat when gently squeezed in your hand and then separate easily with fingers, you are ready to drain whey.

8. Scoop out warm curds using a strainer or clean hands and place them into a colander in the sink. After removing all curds, place the colander on top of warm whey and put the lid on the pot. Allow curds to mat (cheddar) for 10 minutes.

9. Curds should now be one solid slab in the bottom of the colander. Cut slab in half and place one half on top of the other. Cover the pot and allow curds to cheddar for 10 minutes.

10. Flip curd slab over. Cover and allow it to cheddar for another 10 minutes. Continue flipping and covering every 10 minutes for 1 hour.

11. Remove slab from the colander and place on a cutting board. *Mill* curd slab by cutting it into pieces ½×½×2 inches long. Toss milled pieces with salt.

12. Place curds in a zip-lock bag for storage. Curds will keep in the refrigerator for up to 1 week; however, the squeak is strongest right after they are made.

Wisconsin Peanuts

A snack of salty squeaky cheese curd with a cold beer cannot be beat. You can also enjoy these tasty cheese curds with a slice of sweet apple pie and vanilla ice cream.

Ingredients:

1 cup all-purpose flour

1½ tsp. baking powder

1 tsp. salt

½ tsp. black pepper

2 eggs, beaten

½ cup milk or flat beer

1 qt. corn oil for deep frying

1 lb. fresh cheese curds

Yield: *1 pound fried cheese curds*
Prep time: 15 minutes
Cook time: 15 to 20 minutes

1. In a medium bowl, combine flour, baking powder, salt, and pepper. Add eggs and milk or beer and whisk until smooth. If too thick, add extra milk or beer.

2. Heat oil in a deep saucepan to 375°F. Prepare a baking sheet by lining with several layers of paper towels and have ready near the pan of hot oil.

3. Dip each cheese curd into the batter, gently shake off excess, and carefully drop into hot oil. Don't overcrowd. Fry until golden brown, about 1 minute.

4. Remove fried curds with a slotted spoon or strainer and place on prepared baking sheet to drain.

Traditional Cheddar Cheese

Cheddar is a dry, firm cheese with varying degrees of sharpness brought on by aging. Cheddar can be as young as a few months to as old as 9 or more years.

Yield: *3 to 3½ pounds*

Prep time: 6 hours

Rest time: 3 to 12 months

Ingredients:

4 gallons pasteurized whole milk

6 to 12 drops annatto cheese colorant (optional)

2 tsp. prepared calcium chloride solution

¼ tsp. mesophilic culture

½ prepared rennet tablet

5 TB. flaked salt

½ cup water

Equipment:

20-quart (5-gallon) cheese pot

Thermometer

Curd knife

Slotted spoon

Measuring spoons

Colander or strainer

Coarse cheesecloth

Cutting board

Tomme press with weights

Bamboo drying mat

Cheese wax

1. Combine milk, annatto (if using), and calcium chloride in a 20-quart cheese pot. Slowly heat mixture to 86°F. Stir to prevent milk from scorching.

2. Turn off heat and sprinkle culture onto milk surface. Allow culture to rehydrate for 2 or 3 minutes before stirring into milk. Cover the pot and allow to acidify at 86°F for 1 hour.

3. Note the time and add rennet by mixing it into milk with an up-and-down motion for about 1 minute. Let milk set, covered, at 86°F for 45 to 60 minutes or until curd mass shows a clean break. You may elect to use the gel development test described in Chapter 7 to more closely estimate the setting time. Cut gel into ¼-inch cubes. Let curds heal for 5 minutes.

4. Slowly raise the temperature of curds and whey to 100°F over a 30-minute period, increasing the temperature 2°F every 5 minutes, stirring throughout. If you do not have a double boiler that can accommodate the larger cheese pot,

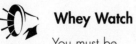

Whey Watch

You must be very gentle when stirring the curds as they heat. Vigorous stirring can cause the curds to release milkfat back into the whey.

place the pot in a sink full of 100°F water. You can gradually raise the temperature of the sink water by adding hot water. A separate pot of boiling water on the stove is handy for adding to the sink. When the temperature of curds has reached 100°F, cover the pot and maintain this temperature for 30 minutes. Stir occasionally to keep curds from matting.

Tasty Chatter

Unlike the Italian-style cheeses which rely on lipase to produce their sharp picante flavor, the sharpness of cheddar is derived from the cheddaring process. Cheddaring aids in removing whey to produce a firmer curd and drier cheese. The process also provides more time for the development of lactic acid, producing the sharp, tangy flavor.

This recipe requires a 20-quart (5-gallon) cheese pot to accommodate the 4 gallons of milk because the cheddaring process will greatly reduce the moisture content of the curds. The larger batch size is needed to produce enough curd to fill the Tomme cheese press so it will function properly.

The cheddaring process begins with Step 4. Read the process through a few times and refer to Chapter 7 to be sure you understand the steps involved. Monitor the temperatures closely.

Curds as they are stirred.

Cheese Bite

Cheddaring is the process by which the drained and matted curd is sliced, stacked, and turned to allow whey to be expelled. This aids in the development of a firmer curd during pressing.

5. Remove the pot from the sink or double boiler and let it rest for 20 more minutes. Pour curds into a large colander to drain. Place the colander over the pot to finish draining for 15 minutes. You should now have one solid mass of curds that stick together.

6. Remove curd mass from the colander and place onto a cutting board. Slice curds into 3×½-inch slabs. Return slabs of curd to cheese pot, covering the bottom with a single layer. Slice and stack another layer on top of the last. Repeat the stacking until all curds are returned to the pot. Place the pot back into a hot water bath and hold the temperature at 100°F for 15 minutes. Turn all stacks over and let rest for 15 more minutes.

Drained cheddar curd ready for slicing.

Restack slabs so that the height of the stack has doubled. Continue flipping stack every 15 minutes for 90 minutes. Note that as time passes stacks will start to knit together, forming thick slabs of rubbery curd. Their texture can be compared to that of a cooked chicken breast.

Stacks of cheddar slabs.

After 90 minutes you will notice a considerable amount of whey in the pot. Slabs will have flattened out and curds should have knitted together to form one solid mass. They will also have a pleasant cheese aroma and tangy flavor.

Cheddar ready for milling.

7. Cut or mill slabs of curd into ½-inch pieces and return to the pot of whey. Hold the temperature of curds at 100°F for 30 minutes. Very gently stir curds with your hands every 10 minutes to keep them from matting together. Carefully tip the pot to drain off remaining whey. Add 4 tablespoons salt, 1 tablespoon at a time, mixing and waiting 1 minute between each addition.

8. Prepare your cheese press as instructed in Chapter 7. Press with 10 pounds of weight for 15 minutes. Turn cheese over and press again with 40 pounds for 12 hours. Turn cheese a third time and press with 50 pounds for 24 hours.

9. Remove cheese from the press as before and unwrap. Mix 1 tablespoon salt with ½ cup water. Using a corner of the cheesecloth, lightly apply saltwater wash to the cheese. Place cheese on a bamboo mat to air dry for 1 to 3 days, turning it over twice each day. When it starts to form a yellowish rind and is dry to the touch, it is ready to wax for storage.

10. Wax cheese as described in Chapter 7 and store for aging at 40°F to 60°F (55°F is ideal) for 3 to 12 months. Turn cheese over daily for the first month and several times a week thereafter.

Cheddar Apple Crisp

The tradition of serving cheddar cheese with apples takes on a new dimension when both are served warm with ice cream.

Ingredients:

5 Granny Smith apples, peeled, cored, and sliced into quarters

1 TB. lemon juice

½ cup + 2 TB. brown sugar

1 tsp. ground cinnamon

½ cup rolled oats

¼ cup flour

⅛ tsp. ground nutmeg

½ cup (1 stick) unsalted butter

½ cup chopped pecans

1 cup (4 oz.) shredded cheddar

Yield: *8 1-cup servings*
Prep time: 30 minutes
Cook time: 30 to 40 minutes

1. Preheat oven to 350°F. Combine sliced apples, lemon juice, ½ cup sugar, and ½ teaspoon cinnamon in a large bowl and toss together. Pour mixture into a buttered 8×8 baking pan.

2. For topping, combine oats, flour, 2 tablespoons brown sugar, ½ teaspoon cinnamon, and nutmeg in a medium bowl. Using your fingers, cut in chilled ½-inch cubes butter until mixture is crumbly. Add pecans and cheddar cheese and mix.

3. Top apples with oat mixture and bake in oven for 30 to 40 minutes or until filling is bubbly and topping is lightly browned.

4. Remove from the oven and allow to cool for 20 minutes. Serve warm with vanilla ice cream.

The Least You Need to Know

- Farmhouse cheddar is a quick cheddar to make that can be eaten immediately.
- The cheddaring process helps to form a firmer curd and a drier cheese.
- "Milling" refers to cutting more precise size pieces of curd.
- Controlling temperature and time is essential in the processing of hard cheeses.

Washed Curd and Brined Cheeses

In This Chapter

- ◆ Treating cheese with salt brine
- ◆ Making Havarti, feta, and provolone
- ◆ Understanding Baby Gouda and Edam
- ◆ Preparing Baby Swiss

This chapter provides recipes for three regional classic cheeses. Each cheese is known for its distinctive shape, aroma, and flavor. You will be using the detailed process of warm washing the curds and the technique of salt brining. The process steps required to make these cheeses are more complex than the previous cheese recipes, but the reward is worth the extra effort.

Brine Treatment

Brining is a wet method of introducing salt into a cheese. During the brining treatment, water (whey) is expelled and salt (sodium chloride) replaces it. This method results in a gradient level of salt being present in the cheese, with the salt concentration higher at the surface than in the center of the cheese.

Whey Watch _____

The heavy brine solution is for one-time use. Once a cheese has been treated in the brine, the calcium and acidity are no longer suitable for use and the mixture must be discarded.

Successful brining is dependent on the condition of the brine in relationship to the cheese. Ideally both the cheese and the brine will be the same temperature, have the same pH, and contain equal amounts of calcium. Calcium chloride is added to the brine to balance the calcium contained in the cheese. Vinegar is added to lower the pH of the brine to more closely match that of the cheese. Without these additions, the rind of the cheese will become soft and gummy and eventually the cheese will lose its shape.

Heavy Brine Formula

This formula for heavy salt brine is used with all the cheeses in this chapter.

Yield: *½ gallon*

Prep time: 15 minutes

Rest time: 1 to 6 hours, depending on cooling method

Ingredients:

½ gallon water

1 lb. flaked salt

1½ tsp. calcium chloride solution

1 to 1½ tsp. white vinegar

1. Prepare heavy brine by combining water with salt. Heat and stir until salt is dissolved.

2. Remove from heat and add calcium chloride along with white vinegar. Stir thoroughly. Allow brine to cool to room temperature.

Cheese Bite _____

Kosher salt may be substituted for flaked pickling salt when preparing the heavy brine. Note that it will take longer to completely dissolve.

The amount of salt the cheese will contain and the depth it reaches inside the cheese are dependent on the original moisture content of the cheese after pressing and the length of time it spent in the brine. Drier curd cheeses will take up less salt than moist curd cheeses. The rind of brine-treated cheese will tend to be firmer and thicker than that of dry salted cheese.

Havarti

Havarti cheese tastes buttery, ranging from somewhat sweet to very sweet, but with a slightly acidic flavor. The typical aging time is around 3 months. In cases where it is aged for a longer period of time, it will become more salty and develop a hazelnut taste.

Ingredients:

1½ tsp. calcium chloride solution

3 gallons whole milk

¼ tsp. mesophilic culture (a mesophilic starter which includes *biovar diacetylactis* is preferred but not required)

½ prepared rennet tablet

3 TB. flaked salt

1 TB. dried dill weed, caraway seeds, or whole cumin (optional)

½ gallon heavy brine

Equipment:

Large pot (at least 6 quarts)

Slotted spoon

Colander or strainer

Cheesecloth

Tomme press with weights

Cheese wax

Kettle of water heated to 165°F to 170°F

Yield: *3 to 3¼ pounds*

Prep time: 2 hours

Rest time: 1½ to 2 months

Cheese Bite

Havarti is a cow's milk cheese that is interior-ripened without a rind and with a smooth surface. It has a bright creamy yellow color, and small, irregular "eyes." Its texture can be supple and flexible. The buttery aroma of Havarti cheese is generally subtle. However, the aroma can be quite sharp in stronger varieties. Havarti can be sliced, grilled, or melted and it tends to soften quickly when left at room temperature.

1. Combine calcium chloride with milk and gently heat to 90°F. Remove from heat.

Tasty Chatter

Hanne Nielsen, the wife of a New Zealand farmer, is the cheesemaker credited with inventing Havarti cheese in the mid-1800s. She traveled throughout Europe learning various cheese-making techniques and secrets. Her finest creation was an original washed-rind cheese she named Havarti, after her farm.

2. Sprinkle culture over milk surface and let rehydrate for 1 or 2 minutes. Gently and thoroughly stir culture into milk. Allow milk to ripen for 30 minutes to 90°F.

3. Note the time and add rennet by mixing it into milk with an up-and-down motion for about 1 minute. Monitor gel development with the method described in Chapter 7, using a rate factor of 3. It should take approximately 15 minutes. After the set time has elapsed, check gel for a clean break.

4. Once you see a clean break, cut gel into ½-inch cubes with a curd knife. It is okay if they are not perfect cubes. Let curds heal for 5 minutes.

5. Gently stir curds for 5 minutes. Cut any oversized chunks into more uniform pieces. Let curds heal and settle for 5 minutes. If curds don't settle, stir for another 5 minutes and allow them to settle again.

6. Pour off about ⅓ of whey (about 1 gallon) by carefully tipping the pot. You may need a free hand or lid to hold back curds. (Whey can be discarded or collected for making ricotta cheese later.)

7. Add 2 quarts of the 170°F wash water and stir. This will raise the temperature of curds and whey to 100°F. Stir in flaked salt. Hold the temperature of curds at 100°F for 30 minutes. This is done by placing the cheese pot in a sink of water with a temperature no higher than 110°F. Stir curds occasionally to keep from matting together. While curds are resting, prepare the cheesecloth for use in pressing cheese.

8. Test curds to see if they will mat or stick together. Take a handful and gently squeeze them together. If they stick together but are easily separated with your fingers, they are ready to drain and press. If they do not mat, let them remain in whey 5 minutes longer and recheck.

9. Place a colander or strainer over a large kettle and pour curds into it. Cover curds so that the heat of the drained whey keeps them warm. (The cheese press will perform better if curds are slightly warm.) Let curds drain for 5 minutes.

10. Using your hands, gently mix curds to separate them. You want curds to be loose when placed into the press. You may wish to add dried dill weed, caraway seeds, or whole cumin at this time for flavor (if using).

11. Load curds into the cheese press as described in Chapter 7. Press with a 10-pound weight for 15 minutes. Remove the weight, follower, and cheesecloth. Turn cheese over and redress it in the cheesecloth. Place cheese back into the press and press with 20 pounds of weight for 15 minutes. Repeat the turning, redressing, and pressing of cheese using 25 to 30 pounds of pressure for 6 hours.

12. After cheese is pressed, remove cheesecloth and place wheel into room-temperature brine for 3 hours. Brine temperature should be the same as the cheese. Cheese will float in the dense brine. Lightly sprinkle flaked salt on its exposed surfaces.

> **Cheese Bite**
> The curds are placed loosely into the cheese press to promote the formation of small eyes.

13. Remove cheese from brine and dry on a bamboo mat or other suitable surface at room temperature until dry to the touch. Do not allow the cheese to become overly dry and form cracks in the rind. Drying can take up to a full day depending on the relative humidity.

14. Once dry, the cheese is ready to be waxed. Prepare the cheese wax as described in Chapter 7. Place finished wheel on the waxed paper and allow the wax to completely cool.

15. Age waxed cheese for 6 to 8 weeks at 50°F to 55°F. If you don't have a separate refrigerator that you can dedicate to aging, place waxed cheese in the warmest section of your refrigerator. This is usually inside of the door near the top. You may need to age cheeses for a longer period if they are stored at a cooler temperature.

Open-Face Ham, Asparagus, and Havarti Sandwich

The buttery flavor of Havarti pairs beautifully with ham and asparagus in this sandwich recipe.

Yield: *2 servings*
Prep time: 30 minutes
Cook time: Less than 1 minute

Ingredients:

4 thin slices pumpernickel rye bread

4 tsp. unsalted butter, softened

8 oz. thinly sliced ham

8 thin stalks asparagus, steamed until crisp tender then chilled

4 thin slices Havarti, cut in half diagonally

1. Lay bread out and spread a thin layer of butter on each slice. Divide ham evenly among bread slices, folding or trimming it to fit bread. Cut each open-face sandwich in half diagonally and place onto a baking sheet.

2. Preheat the broiler. Cut asparagus in half and divide evenly among sandwiches. Lay one piece of Havarti over each sandwich half. Place the tray under the broiler briefly to soften cheese, about 20 to 30 seconds. Remove immediately.

3. Garnish with fresh dill tips and serve with grainy mustard.

Baby Gouda

This recipe presents an option for making two different cheeses, Gouda and Edam, using the same process. The difference between Gouda and Edam is the amount of milkfat they contain. Gouda is made with whole milk, resulting in a finished cheese with about 48 percent milkfat. Edam is made using part-skimmed milk, which results in 40 percent milkfat. The recipe given here is for a small batch of traditionally shaped Baby Gouda. All that is necessary to make Edam cheese is to replace the whole milk with 2 percent milk.

Although larger-size Gouda can improve from aging over many months under specific storage conditions, the miniature version called Baby Gouda is meant to be eaten young. The cheese will still benefit from aging 2 to 6 months.

Ingredients:

1 gallon whole milk

⅛ tsp. mesophilic culture (a mesophilic starter which includes *biovar diacetylactis* is preferred but not required)

½ tsp. calcium chloride solution

¼ prepared rennet tablet

Equipment:

Large pot (at least 6 quarts)

Slotted spoon

Colander or strainer

Cheesecloth

2 Baby Gouda molds with weights

½ gallon heavy brine

Cheese wax

Kettle of water heated to 170°F

Yield: *2 8-ounce Baby Gouda wheels*

Prep time: 24 hours

Rest time: 2 to 6 months

1. In a 6-quart or larger pot, gently heat milk to 90°F. Remove from heat.

2. Sprinkle culture over milk surface and let rehydrate for 1 or 2 minutes. Gently and thoroughly stir culture into milk.

3. Add calcium chloride and stir into milk.

Tasty Chatter

You will note that making Gouda is very similar to making Havarti. The key difference is that Gouda employs a multi-step warm-washing method to produce the texture and mild flavor you expect from young Gouda.

4. Note the time and add rennet by mixing it into milk with an up-and-down motion for about 1 minute. Monitor gel development with the method described in Chapter 7, using a rate factor of 3. After the set time has elapsed, check gel for a clean break.

5. When gel shows a clean break, use a curd knife to cut curds into ½-inch pieces. It is okay if they are not perfect cubes. Let curds heal for 5 minutes.

6. Gently stir curds for 5 minutes. Cut any oversized pieces into more uniform pieces. Let curds heal and settle for 10 minutes. If curds don't settle after 10 minutes, stir another 5 minutes and allow them to settle to the bottom.

7. Stir in 1 cup 175°F water from the kettle of water. This will quickly raise the curd temperature. Stir gently for 10 minutes. Whey temperature should be 93°F to 94°F. Let curds settle for 10 minutes. While curds settle, adjust the temperature of the hot water kettle to 150°F to 155°F. Add cold water if it's too hot.

Cheese Bite

If Baby Gouda molds are unavailable, you can make enough curds to use the Tomme press. The process and brine recipe will remain the same. This version will yield a 3-pound wheel of cheese:

Large Gouda wheel ingredients:

3 gallons whole milk

¼ tsp. mesophilic culture as described previously

1½ tsp. calcium chloride solution

½ prepared rennet tablet

8. Pour off a measured 3½ to 4 cups of whey by carefully tipping the pot. You may need a free hand or lid to hold back curds. (Whey can be discarded or collected for making ricotta cheese later.)

9. Replace measured volume of whey with an equal volume of 150°F to 155°F hot water. Stir curds gently. You may need to adjust the temperature of the water you add so that the final temperature in the cheese pot is 100°F. Keep curds at 100°F for 20 minutes. Stir occasionally.

10. Prepare cheesecloth for use in pressing cheese.

11. Test curds to see if they will mat together. If they do not mat, let them stay in whey 5 minutes longer and recheck.

12. Place a colander or strainer over a large kettle and pour curds into it. Cover curds so that the heat of the drained whey keeps them warm. (Curds will press better if slightly warm.) Let curds drain for 5 minutes.

13. Line the Baby Gouda molds with cheesecloth. Divide curds equally between the molds. Fold the cheesecloth over curds and place followers on top. Press with a 1-pound weight on top of each for 15 minutes. Be careful to keep the press and follower level. This will ensure that the traditional Gouda shape is formed.

Cheese Bite

Four rolls of pennies make a great weight since together they equal about 1 pound.

14. Remove the weights and follower. Carefully lift each cheese out of the mold by the cheesecloth. Unwrap cheeses and turn over. Redress with the cheesecloth and place back into the molds. Replace the followers and press with 2 to 3 pounds for 15 minutes.

15. Repeat turning, redressing, and pressing cheeses using 2 to 3 pounds of pressure. It can take up to 4 turnings for rinds to become fairly smooth without any gaps between curds.

Whey Watch

When using Baby Gouda molds, it is best to apply pressure with low-profile thin weights. Stacking weights or using tall objects such as canned goods may cause the follower to tip, ruining the shape of the cheese.

16. When rinds are smooth, leave wrapped cheeses in the presses with 2- to 3-pound weights on them overnight or up to 16 hours. Prepare heavy brine as described at the beginning of this chapter.

17. After cheeses are pressed, remove cheesecloth and place wheels in brine for 2 hours. The temperature of the brine should be the same as the cheese. Cheeses will float in the dense brine. Lightly sprinkle flaked salt on their exposed surfaces.

18. Remove cheeses from brine and dry on a bamboo mat or other suitable surface at room temperature until dry to the touch. Do not allow them to become overly dry and form cracks in the rind. Drying can take up to a full day depending on the relative humidity.

19. Once dry, cheeses are ready to be waxed as described in Chapter 7.

20. Age waxed cheeses for up to 6 months at 50°F to 55°F. If you don't have a separate refrigerator that you can dedicate to aging, place waxed cheese in the warmest section of your refrigerator. You may need to age cheeses for a longer period if they are stored at a cooler temperature.

Apple Gouda Salad

It is recommended that you prepare this recipe just before serving. If made ahead of time, toss apple slices with some of the dressing first to prevent browning.

Yield: *4 1¼-cup servings*

Prep time: 20 minutes

Ingredients:

¼ cup mayonnaise

2 tsp. lemon juice

Salt and black pepper

2 sweet red apples quartered, cored, and thinly sliced

2 cups thinly sliced celery

1 cup Gouda cut into ½-inch cubes

Boston lettuce leaves for garnish

½ cup chopped walnuts

1. In a medium bowl, combine mayonnaise, lemon juice, and salt and pepper to taste.

2. Add apples, celery, and cheese to dressing and stir to coat.

3. Line 4 chilled plates with lettuce leaves and divide salad evenly among them.

4. Garnish with chopped walnuts.

Feta Cheese

This classic Greek cheese dates back thousands of years. Its salty flavor and dry texture works well in cold salads and acts as a high-protein seasoning in hot, savory dishes.

Ingredients:

1 gallon whole milk (goat's or cow's)

½ tsp. calcium chloride solution

⅛ tsp. mild lipase powder

¼ tsp. mesophilic culture

½ prepared rennet tablet

½ gallon heavy brine

Pickling brine ingredients:

1 quart hot water

3 oz. flaked salt

¾ teaspoon calcium chloride solution

½ teaspoon vinegar

Equipment:

Cheese pot (6-quart or larger)

Slotted spoon

Curd knife

Ladle

2 stackable ricotta baskets

Yield: *16 to 18 ounces*	
Prep time: 6 hours	
Rest time: 18 hours	

1. Prepare lipase powder as described in Chapter 8. Combine milk with calcium chloride and lipase powder in a 6-quart or larger pot. Gently stir milk as it heats to 90°F. Remove the pot from heat.

2. Sprinkle culture over milk surface and let rehydrate for 1 or 2 minutes. Gently and thoroughly stir culture into milk.

3. Note the time and add rennet by mixing it into milk with an up-and-down motion for about 1 minute. Monitor gel development with the method described in Chapter 7, using a rate factor of 4. After the set time has elapsed, check gel for a clean break.

4. Use a curd knife to cut curds into ½-inch pieces. It is okay if they are not perfect cubes. Let curds heal for 5 minutes.

Tasty Chatter

Traditional feta is made from goat's milk or a combination of goat's and sheep's milk. Most of the feta sold today is made of cow's milk. Along with the use of lipase powder, making feta cheese requires a two-step brining process. First, the cheese is soaked in a heavy saltwater brine to develop the rind. Secondly, the cheese is stored in a lighter pickling brine to protect it from exposure to air and to preserve it.

---

5. Maintaining the temperature at 90°F, stir curds gently for 20 minutes. Allow curds to settle for 10 minutes.

6. Drain whey into the sink, holding curds back with your free hand. Use a ladle or coffee cup to scoop curds into the ricotta baskets.

7. Place one basket on a tray to catch whey. Place the other on top of the first. Allow cheese to press for 30 minutes.

8. Remove the top basket, turn cheese over in each of the baskets, and switch them, placing the bottom basket on top. Press for another 30 minutes.

9. Repeat this flipping and switching sequence two more times, allowing 1 full hour between switches. The total time will equal 3 hours of pressing.

 Cheese Bite _____

Ricotta baskets look like small colanders. A handy substitute would be berry baskets, like the plastic pint-size ones that strawberries come in. An alternative to using a basket is to drain the curd in a cheesecloth-lined colander. Wrap the curds with the cheesecloth and set in a draining tray. Use the pressing method employed in the Paneer recipe from Chapter 4. Press with a light 2-pound weight for 3 hours.

10. Remove cheeses from the baskets and place on a draining mat. Cover loosely with cheese cloth. Allow to dry overnight at room temperature. Prepare heavy brine as described at the beginning of this chapter. Brine must be the same temperature as cheese before use.

11. The next day, cut each cheese into 1½- to 2-inch cubes and place them into heavy brine. Store in the refrigerator for 6 hours. Meanwhile, combine pickling brine ingredients and stir until the salt is dissolved. Place pickling brine in the refrigerator.

Feta cubes ready for pickling.

12. After 6 hours, remove cheese from heavy brine. It will have formed a firm rind. Place blocks of cheese into a clean 1-quart jar and fill with pickling brine. Brine should completely fill the jar. Place a lid on the jar and store in the refrigerator. The feta is ready to eat after spending 24 hours in pickling brine to reach a salt equilibrium, but will continue to increase in sharpness as it ages for up to 1 year. The temperature for aging can be anywhere from your regular refrigerator temperature up to 55°F.

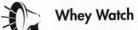

Whey Watch

Make sure the cubes stay submerged in the pickling brine. When feta cheese is exposed to air in the pickling jar, it may develop mold.

Frittata with Tomato, Canadian Bacon, and Feta Cheese

This recipe combines an eclectic mix of flavors and textures for a savory brunch or lunch dish.

Yield: *4 to 6 servings*
Prep time: 15 minutes
Cook time: 10 to 15 minutes

Ingredients:

6 large eggs

1 TB. water

1 TB. olive oil

4 slices Canadian bacon, diced into ¼-inch pieces (about ½ cup)

½ cup chopped and seeded plum tomato

1 cup crumbled feta cheese

¼ cup fresh basil chiffonade

1. Turn on the oven broiler. Beat eggs and water with wire whisk in a medium bowl.

2. Heat an ovenproof 9-inch skillet over medium heat. When skillet is hot, add the oil and Canadian bacon and sauté for 1 minute.

3. Turn heat down to medium-low and add beaten egg mixture. Sprinkle chopped tomato and ½ cup feta cheese evenly over top of eggs.

4. Let eggs cook without disturbing them until they are about ⅔ cooked through. It will help to place a lid over the skillet. You want the bottom of the frittata to be set with a thin layer of uncooked egg on top. Adjust heat if bottom is browning too quickly.

5. Carefully place the skillet under the broiler and finish cooking top of frittata for 1 to 3 minutes or until eggs are puffy and no longer shiny on top. Watch closely so you do not overbrown the top. Remove from oven and top with remaining feta and basil chiffonade. Cut into wedges and serve warm.

Tasty Chatter

Chiffonade simply means cut into long strips or ribbons. For basil chiffonade, stack the leaves and roll them tightly then cut across the roll to make elegant strips.

Provolone

Provolone falls into the pasta filata category of cheeses because of the curd-stretching technique used to develop its elastic stringy texture. The flavor of provolone cheese can range from mild and sweet to very sharp, depending on the type of lipase powder used and the amount of time the cheese has been aged.

Ingredients:

1 gallon whole milk

¼ tsp. thermophilic culture

½ tsp. calcium chloride solution

¼ tsp. mild lipase powder

¼ prepared rennet tablet

½ gallon heavy brine

Equipment:

Cheese pot (6-quart or larger)

Extra pot or tea kettle for hot water

Thermometer

Curd knife

Slotted spoon

Measuring spoons

Colander or strainer

2 2- to 3-quart bowls

6- to 8-foot butcher's string

Heat-proof gloves for curd stretching (optional)

pH meter to determine when to stretch curds (optional)

Yield: *1 pound*
Prep time: 4 hours
Rest time: 2 to 6 months

1. In a 6-quart or larger cheese pot, gently heat milk to 97°F. Remove from heat.

2. Sprinkle culture over milk surface and let rehydrate for 1 or 2 minutes. Gently and thoroughly stir culture into milk. Let milk ripen for 1 hour.

3. Add calcium chloride and lipase powder and stir into milk. Let cheese milk rest for 10 minutes.

4. Note the time and add rennet by mixing into milk with an up-and-down motion for about 1 minute. Monitor gel development with the method described in Chapter 7, using a rate factor of 3.5. After the set time has elapsed, check gel for a clean break.

> **Tasty Chatter**
>
> Provolone cheese uses thermophilic starter cultures due to the temperatures used in processing the curd. Using nonhomogenized milk will give superior results when it is time to stretch the cheese.

5. When gel shows a clean break, use a curd knife to cut curds into ¼-inch pieces. It is okay if they are not perfect cubes. Let curds heal for 5 minutes.

6. Gently stir curds and whey over low heat, raising the temperature 2°F every 5 minutes until whey reaches 118°F. This should take 45 minutes.

7. Place a colander or strainer over a large pot and pour curds into it. Place a lid over curds so that the heat of the drained whey keeps them warm. Allow curds to drain until ready to stretch. It will take anywhere from 45 to 90 minutes.

8. To facilitate whey drainage and lactic acid production, place the pot of draining curds into a 110°F sink of water and maintain curd temperature. Or place the pot on the stove and intermittently turn the burner on for short periods of time to maintain the warmth.

9. Meanwhile, heat about 2 quarts water to between 170°F and 180°F using a separate pot or tea kettle. Fill a bowl with 2 quarts ice water (to chill cheese when finished).

10. Thirty minutes into the draining time, begin to test for stretchability. Pinch off 2 small pieces of curd about the size of gumballs and place into a mixing bowl. Ladle a cup of hot water over them and wait for 1 minute. Use 2 spoons or your gloved hands to knead balls of cheese together below the surface of the hot water until they come together and are soft and pliable. Pick up cheese and attempt to stretch into a long thread. When it stretches into a shiny string, the whole cheese is ready to stretch. If cheese will not join back together and stretch, place it back into the colander. Wait another 10 minutes and test again. You may have to test several times before it is ready.

11. When cheese is ready to stretch, remove from the colander and place on a cutting surface. Cut cheese slab into 1-inch cubes and place into the bowl. Ladle hot water over them to cover. Wait 2 minutes and begin to knead cubes together. Continue kneading until you create one mass of cheese.

Cheese Bite

A pH meter is not necessary for this recipe, but it does take the guesswork out of determining when to stretch the curd. If using one, the target pH is 5.1.

12. Gather cheese into a ball, remove it from hot water, and begin to stretch. Pull cheese into a long rope, loop it back, and pull again. Repeat until rope is long and shiny. If curd breaks, it is cooling too quickly—place cheese back into hot water. You may need to ladle additional hot water into the bowl to increase the temperature.

13. After stretching cheese and forming it into your desired shape, place it into the bowl of prepared ice water for 20 to 30 minutes or until it firms up.

14. Remove cheese from ice water and place it into prepared brine. Keep cheese in brine for 2 hours.

15. Remove cheese from brine and place on a drying mat at room temperature until dry to the touch. Cover cheese loosely with cheesecloth to keep away pests and continue drying for 1 or 2 days.

16. You may elect to hang cheese for aging. This is done by tying cheese in a cradle made of butcher's string.

    Find the center of a 5-foot-long piece of string by folding it in half. Unfold the string and place it on a table top. Place cheese on the center point of string.

    Lift the strings at the same time, holding them as close to cheese as possible. Bring the strings together at top of cheese and cross them. Keeping the string pulled tight, turn the string 90 degrees. Flip cheese over and cross string on opposite side, as if wrapping a gift.

    Continue wrapping and flipping until cheese is divided into eight parts with the string. It will look like a pumpkin.

    When you have formed the eight sections, firmly tie a knot on top of cheese. Slip one end of string under all of the strings and pull it through. (Cheese will be pliable, so this should not be difficult.) Cheese will now be secure for hanging in its string basket.

17. Hang cheese in an aging refrigerator at 50°F to 60°F with 85 percent relative humidity. Dry age the cheese this way for 2 to 3 weeks as a firm rind forms. When rind has

Cheese Bite

As an alternative to hanging the cheese, provolone can be waxed and aged for up to 6 months using the method described in Chapter 7.

formed, rub olive oil on cheese surface to keep rind from drying out too much. The oil will also discourage mold growth. If mold does appear at any time during aging, wipe it away with a damp piece of cheesecloth dipped into flaked salt. Allow cheese to cure for 2 to 6 months.

> **Cheese Bite** _____
>
> A dry-aged provolone is perfect for hanging in a cold smoker to create a classic smoked cheese. Cold smoking is a low-temperature process that will not break down the integrity of the cheese by melting it. The cheese will take on a nice smoked character in as little time as 1 hour.

Antipasto Appetizer Skewers

This is a twist on the typically plated antipasto salad.

Yield: *8 skewers or servings*

Prep time: 60 minutes

Ingredients:

½ cup extra-virgin olive oil

3 TB. balsamic vinegar

1 TB. minced fresh thyme or oregano (1 tsp. dried)

¼ tsp. salt

⅛ tsp. black pepper

8 1-inch cubes Genoa salami

8 large, pitted black olives

8 cremini or button mushrooms

4 paper-thin slices prosciutto

8 1-inch cubes provolone

8 1-inch cubes or balls ripe melon (cantaloupe, honeydew, etc.), chilled

8 wooden or decorative skewers at least 6 inches long

1. In a small bowl, whisk together oil, vinegar, herbs, salt, and pepper. Add salami, olives, and mushrooms and marinate for 30 minutes in refrigerator.

2. Meanwhile, slice prosciutto in half lengthwise, making 8 pieces. Loosely wrap prosciutto around cube of provolone and secure with a skewer.

3. Remove salami, olives, and mushrooms from marinade. Place one of each onto the skewer, including chilled melon, and serve.

Baby Swiss

This final recipe will require all of your newly acquired cheese-making skills. Making a full-size Swiss cheese is outside the hobby cheesemaker's capacity, but you will find this recipe can produce a Baby Swiss with all the flavor and character of an Alpine cheese. Baby Swiss cheese is noted for its creamy texture and pungent flavor.

Ingredients:

3 gallons whole milk

½ tsp. thermophilic culture

1 tsp. *Propionic shermanii* powder

1½ tsp. calcium chloride solution

½ prepared rennet tablet

½ gallon heavy brine

Equipment:

Cheese pot (16-quart or larger)

Thermometer

Curd knife or long wire whisk

Slotted spoon

Measuring spoons

Tomme cheese press with weights

Coarse cheesecloth

Draining mat

12-quart plastic storage box with lid

Mushroom or short, plastic-bristled brush (optional)

Yield: *2¾ to 3 pounds*

Prep time: 4 hours up to pressing

Rest time: 1 day pressing, 18 hours brining, 3 days drying, 2 weeks for eye formation, 3 to 6 months aging

---

1. In a 16-quart or larger cheese pot, gently heat milk to 92°F. Remove from heat.

2. Sprinkle starter and *Propionic shermanii* over milk surface and let rehydrate for 1 or 2 minutes. Gently and thoroughly stir cultures into milk and let milk ripen for 30 minutes.

3. Add calcium chloride and stir it into cheese milk.

4. Note the time and add rennet by mixing it into milk with an up-and-down motion for about 1 minute. Monitor gel development with the method described in Chapter 7, using a rate factor of 3. After the set time has elapsed, check gel for a clean break.

5. When gel shows a clean break, use a curd knife to cut curds into a ¼-inch grid. Use a long-handled wire whisk to continue cutting curds. You want pieces the size of peas. Let curds heal for 5 minutes.

6. Gently stir curds and whey for 1 hour, maintaining the temperature of 90°F.

7. Slowly heat curds to 115°F while stirring over a period of 45 to 50 minutes. Do not increase the temperature by more than 2°F every 5 minutes.

8. Check curds for matting by scooping some into your hand, closing and opening your fist to see if they stick together and then are easily separated with your thumb. If they do not mat, remove the cheese pot from heat and continue stirring for 5 minutes, then recheck.

9. Prepare the cheese press by lining with clean cheesecloth. Carefully pour excess whey into the sink without losing curds. Let the sink drain and then place the press in it. You will need to work quickly to keep curds warm while they press. Ladle curds from the cheese pot into the lined press. If you can't scoop remaining curds from whey, pour whey through a colander or strainer and then add curds to the press.

10. Press cheese with 10 pounds of weight for 30 minutes. Turn cheese and press with 10 pounds for 30 minutes. Turn cheese and press with 20 pounds for 2 hours. Turn again and press with 20 pounds for at least 12 hours or overnight.

11. Meanwhile, prepare brine formula. Heat and stir until salt is dissolved. Allow brine to cool to room temperature as cheese presses overnight.

12. The next day, remove cheese from the press, unwrap it, and place in brine. Refrigerate brine and cheese for 14 to 18 hours or overnight. Halfway through the brining time, turn cheese over in the water.

13. The next day, remove cheese from brine; lightly wipe it with a clean, slightly damp cheesecloth that has been dipped in flaked salt. Place a draining mat on a plate or tray and place cheese on the mat. Refrigerate cheese for 3 days, allowing it to air dry and begin rind formation. Turn cheese 2 times per day. Blot up any moisture that may have collected on the tray.

14. After 3 days, place cheese and draining mat into a sanitized plastic container with a lid. Store this container at room temperature (68°F to 72°F) for 2 to 3 weeks to allow eye formation. Eye formation is underway when cheese begins to puff up slightly with gas. During this time, you will need to turn cheese daily and wipe its surface with a salted piece of cheesecloth. If the conditions are too humid and you notice mold growth, open the lid of the storage container a bit to decrease the humidity. Wipe any moisture from inside the box, including the lid. Gently scrub the mold off of cheese with the salted cheesecloth.

15. Transfer cheese to an aging refrigerator at 45°F to 50°F and 85 percent relative humidity. Age cheese for 3 to 6 months. Turn cheese every other day and continue to remove surface mold with the salted cheesecloth or a mushroom brush.

Whey Watch

The brine used for Swiss cheese differs from the heavy brine used in previous recipes. No calcium or vinegar adjustment is necessary.

Cauliflower Baby Swiss Soup

This easy-to-prepare, flavorful soup is especially good when made with fresh local cauliflower available in the autumn.

Yield: *8 12-ounce servings*

Prep time: 30 minutes

Cook time: 30 to 40 minutes

Ingredients:

4 cups low-salt chicken stock or broth

1 large head cauliflower, cut into ½- to 1-inch pieces

4 TB. unsalted butter

1 large onion, diced

1 tsp. salt

½ tsp. ground black pepper

½ tsp. dry mustard

4 TB. flour

3 cups water

1 cup half-and-half

2 cups grated Baby Swiss cheese

Crumbled bacon and chives for garnish (optional)

1. In a 2½-quart or larger pot, bring chicken broth to a boil. Add cauliflower pieces to pot, turn down heat, and simmer until tender, about 15 to 20 minutes.

2. Meanwhile, in a 4-quart pot or Dutch oven, melt butter over medium-low heat. Add onion, salt, black pepper, and dry mustard and sauté until onions are softened, about 15 minutes.

3. Add flour and turn up heat to medium. Cook and stir 2 minutes more.

4. Slowly add water to the pot, stirring constantly with a wire whisk until evenly mixed. Continue stirring and bring mixture to a boil. Boil for 1 minute. Turn heat back down to medium-low and continue to cook and stir for 5 minutes.

5. Carefully add cauliflower and broth to flour, water, and onion mixture and stir to combine. Turn heat off and stir in half-and-half. Add shredded cheese and stir in until completely melted. Return to low heat, if needed, to completely melt cheese.

6. Serve, garnished with crumbled bacon and chives.

Cheese Bite

Add roasted cauliflower for a hint of sweetness and florets of roasted red pepper for color. Serve in a sourdough bread bowl with a cold glass of fresh apple cider for a complete meal.

What to Do with All That Cheese

It is inevitable that a well-stocked cheese cave will eventually contain remnants of various cheeses. This is especially true for the hobby cheesemaker. These recipes are the perfect way to show off your cheese creations with classic style and flare. It will also free up some room for you to get started on your next great cheese-making project!

The Ultimate Cheese and Macaroni

The ultimate comfort food is updated with your creativity. Use some of your soft cheese in the sauce and then layer in plenty of your favorite hard cheese(s) in the middle and on top of the macaroni.

Ingredients:

¼ cup (½ stick) unsalted butter

¼ cup flour

1 quart milk

¼ lb. soft cheese (chèvre or fromage blanc)

¼ lb. (1 cup) firm cheese, shredded (provolone, Pepper Jack, cheddar, etc.)

Salt and pepper

1 lb. elbow macaroni (or other suitable pasta)

1 lb. (4 cups) combination of firm cheeses, shredded (provolone, Pepper Jack, cheddar, etc.)

2 oz. grated Parmesan cheese

Yield: *8 to 10 1½-cup servings*
Prep time: 30 minutes
Bake time: 1 hour

1. Preheat oven to 350°F. In a 4- to 6-quart pot, melt butter over medium-low heat. Add flour, stir and cook for 1 minute.

2. Gradually add milk while whisking to prevent lumps. Raise heat to medium to bring mixture to a boil. Turn heat down to low and simmer for 5 minutes, whisking often.

3. Remove pot from heat and add soft cheese and ¼ pound shredded cheese, whisking in until smooth. Salt and pepper to taste.

4. Cook pasta according to package instructions; however, stop cooking while pasta is still slightly firm. It will continue to cook in the oven. Drain pasta and add to the pot containing cheese sauce. Mix thoroughly.

5. Butter a 4-quart casserole. Pour half of pasta mixture into the casserole. Top with ½ pound shredded cheeses. Pour remaining pasta mixture on top and finish with remaining shredded cheese.

6. Cover casserole with foil and bake for 35 to 40 minutes. Remove foil, sprinkle grated Parmesan on top and return to the oven until lightly brown, about 10 minutes.

7. Serve garnished with sliced tomatoes, basil, and crusty garlic bread.

Breakfast Cheese Strata

Enjoy your homemade cheese baked into a bread pudding with ham or bacon.

Yield: *6 to 8 1-cup servings*

Prep time: 4½ hours or overnight

Cook time: 1 hour

Ingredients:

10 to 12 slices (¾ lb.) firm white bread, cut or torn into 1-inch pieces

¾ lb. (3 cups) firm cheese, shredded

7 eggs, lightly beaten

3 cups whole milk

1 tsp. dry mustard

⅛ tsp. black pepper

¼ lb. smoked ham or Canadian bacon, cubed

½ cup sliced green onion

1. Generously butter a 13×9 baking pan. Place bread pieces and cheese in pan and arrange evenly.

2. In a large bowl, beat together eggs, milk, dry mustard, black pepper, ham or bacon, and green onion until milk is incorporated. Pour over bread and cheese. Cover and refrigerate for 4 hours or overnight.

3. Preheat oven to 325°F. Uncover the pan and bake strata for 50 to 60 minutes or until custard is set and golden brown.

The Least You Need to Know

♦ Gouda uses whole milk and Edam part-skimmed milk; otherwise they are the same cheese.

♦ Brine is a wet method used to salt cheese.

♦ The flavor of provolone cheese varies depending on the type of lipase powder used and the amount of time the cheese has been aged.

♦ Baby Swiss is an advanced-level cheese for the home cheesemaker to make.

Glossary

acidity   The degree to which a substance furnishes hydrogen ions; having a pH of less than 7. Acidity can be a measured factor during the cheese-making process and also refers to the tanginess present in the flavor of a finished cheese.

aged   Generally a cheese that has been cured longer than 6 months.

alkalinity   Having a pH of more than 7.

ambient temperature   The temperature in a room, or the temperature that surrounds an object under discussion.

amino acids   Chemical substances found in foods that are commonly called the building blocks of protein. Nutritionally, essential amino acids are released into the bloodstream during the digestion of cheese curd.

anaerobic   Absence of oxygen. Most cheese making requires an anaerobic fermentation or aging period.

annatto   A natural vegetable dye used to give many cheese varieties a yellow-orange hue.

bacteria   A large group of one-celled microorganisms widely distributed in nature that are used in cheese making.

baker's formula   A bulk recipe where the secondary ingredients are expressed as a percentage of the weight of the primary ingredient (flour).

bitter   An unpleasant, biting aftertaste. Caused in cheese by excessive use of rennet and/or tainted milk.

body   The physical attributes of cheese when touched, handled, cut, or eaten.

brine   In cheese making, the nearly saturated solution of salt in water used as a means of salting cheese.

brining   A step in cheese making where the whole cheese is floated in a brine solution.

calcium   An alkaline element that occurs in milk, vegetables, and egg yolks.

calcium chloride   A calcium salt used in cheese making to aid coagulation.

casein   The principal protein in milk.

cheddaring   The curd-processing method used to develop the flavor and texture of cheddar cheese prior to pressing.

cheese   The product obtained when the milk protein casein is coagulated by an enzyme and/or acid-producing bacteria.

cheesecloth   A thin, loosely woven cloth of cotton used in cheese making or for straining liquids.

chèvre   The French word for "goat," commonly used to refer to all cheeses made of goat's milk.

chymosin   An enzyme from the stomach that clots milk. Also known as rennin.

citric acid   An acidulant contained in various fruits and made synthetically.

coagulant   A rennetlike enzyme, also used commercially, produced by selected fungi and bacteria. *See also* rennet.

coagulation   The aggregation of protein macromolecules into clumps or aggregates of semi-solid material called curd.

coliforms   Commonly used bacterial indicator of the sanitary quality of food and water.

colloid   A mixture in which one substance is divided into minute particles (called colloidal particles) and dispersed throughout a second substance. The permanent suspension of microscopic fat globules makes milk a colloid.

creamery   An establishment where dairy products are prepared or sold.

crème fraîche   A type of thick cream made from heavy cream with the addition of buttermilk, sour cream, or yogurt.

curd knife   Any suitable straight edge used to cleanly cut curds into uniform pieces.

curds   The solid portion of coagulated milk.

degree of resolution   A reference to the accuracy of a measurement. For example, a pH meter that is calibrated in $\frac{1}{10}$ increments is more accurate than pH strips that measure in whole increments.

denaturing   A change in a protein molecule, usually by an unfolding of the amino acid chains, with a decrease in solubility. Denatured milk protein will not respond naturally when exposed to a coagulating enzyme.

diacetyl   The flavor-aroma agent in butter, formed during the ripening stage by the organism *Lactococcus lactis cremoris*.

distillation   Process in which a liquid is purified by vaporizing, condensing, and collecting the resulting liquid.

emulsification   The process of dispersing one liquid in a second incompatible liquid such as vinegar or oil.

enzymes   Catalysts produced by living cells. They are composed of protein and destroyed by heat and protein coagulation. *See* rennet.

fat content   The amount of fat in a cheese, determined by analyzing the fat in the dry matter and expressed as a percentage of the entire dry matter.

fermentation   Changes in food caused by intentional growth of bacteria, yeast, or mold. The function performed by a cheese starter culture.

flocculation   The first visible signs of coagulation. Usually occurs about 10 minutes after rennet is added to milk.

gel   A colloidal dispersion that shows some rigidity or moldability at room temperature. Occurs when the addition of rennet to milk causes the protein to form a solid mass of curd.

GMO   Genetically modified organism. The acronym can apply to plants, animals, or microorganisms.

herd share   An arrangement in which the consumer pays a farmer a fee for boarding and caring for his share of a cow, goat, etc. The cow shareowner then obtains the milk from his own animal.

homogenize   To reduce the particles of a substance (specifically milk) so that they are uniformly small and evenly distributed.

hydrolyse   In cheese making, it is the breakdown of fats into the fatty acids that produce the distinctive flavor and aroma of strong Italian and alpine cheeses. *See* lipase.

inoculation   To introduce a microorganism into a suitable situation for growth. In cheese making, this refers to the introduction of a starter culture to milk.

ions   A group of atoms that carries a positive or negative electric charge as a result of having lost or gained one or more electrons.

lactic acid   The acid produced by the fermentation of milk sugar (lactose).

lactose   A sugar naturally occurring in milk, also known as "milk sugar," that is the least sweet of all natural sugars.

lipase   Enzyme that hydrolyzes fat to glycerol and fatty acid to produce a sharp flavor.

matrix   A collection arranged into a fixed number of rows and columns. Caused when casein micelles (amino acid chains) reverse the reaction from polar (repelling each other) to attraction; the matrix entraps the surrounding milkfat globules along with the bacteria starter and water.

mesophilic bacteria   Bacteria that grows best at moderate temperatures of 77°F to 86°F.

micelle   A submicroscopic collection of molecules into spheres due to their electric polarity. When the polarity of the liquid surrounding the micelles is changed by acidification or the addition of an enzyme, the micelles will attract and coagulate into curd.

microflora   Living microorganisms that are so small that they can be seen only with a microscope and that maintain a more or less constant presence in a particular area, such as the pharynx or the rumen.

milkfat   Also called butterfat. The fat content of milk expressed as a percentage of the total weight.

milling   Process of cutting large slabs of curd into small, uniform pieces in preparation for pressing.

mold   Fungi used in the ripening of cheese (species of *Penicillium*) and as the source of enzymes.

nonfat dry milk   Powder obtained from pasteurized skim milk after water is removed through a drying process.

organic   Term once used as an adjective to identify anything containing carbon. Currently defines agricultural products that are grown using cultural, biological, and mechanical methods prior to the use of synthetic, nonagricultural substances to control pests, improve soil quality, and/or enhance processing.

Parmigiano-Reggiano   A hard grating cheese from the Parma region of Italy, made from raw cow's milk.

pasta filata   Translated literally from Italian, it means "to spin pasta or threads." Pasta filata refers to cheeses where curds are heated and then stretched or kneaded before being molded into the desired shape.

pasteurization   Heating of a specific food enough to destroy the most heat-resistant pathogenic or disease-causing microorganisms known to be associated with that food.

pathogens   Microorganisms that cause infectious disease by invading the body of an organism known as the host.

Penicillium candidum   The white mold used to ripen and flavor Brie, Camembert, and a variety of French goat cheeses.

pH   A numerical scale from 1 to 14 indicating the degree of acidity; 1 is most acid, 7 is neutral, and 14 is most alkaline.

pharmaceutical grade   Of a standard suitable for use as a medicine.

picante   Spicy, biting, or sharp flavor.

precipitate   The solid portion of curds and whey.

protein   Essential components of all living cells (along with fats and carbohydrates). Proteins are composed of carbon, hydrogen, oxygen, nitrogen, sulfur, and sometimes phosphorus. All proteins are composed of large combinations of 20 amino acids.

queso   The Spanish word for cheese.

raw milk   Milk that is not treated or processed.

rennet   An extract from the membranes of calves' stomachs that contains rennin. *See also* coagulant.

rennin   An enzyme that aids in coagulating milk or separating curds from whey.

ricotta basket   A plastic basket used to drain ricotta cheese, leaving a basket-weave impression on the curd.

ripening of cheese   Process of aging cheese in which degradation of lactose, proteins, and fat are carried out by ripening agents such as bacteria, enzymes, rennet, molds, or yeasts.

ripening of milk   Process after inoculation in which bacteria produce lactic acid, thereby developing acidity before the addition of rennet.

scalding   Exposing a liquid to a sudden increase in temperature hot enough to burn.

sharp   A descriptive term for cheese with a pleasant tang and sour flavor due to a concentration of acid. By contrast, a cheese with biting sting or sour taste indicates an excessive concentration of acid, which is a defect.

slurry   A thin mixture of water and a fine insoluble material.

starter culture   A culture that normally consists of varying percentages of lactic acid bacteria or mold spores, enzymes, or other microorganisms and natural chemicals that is used to speed and control the process of curdling milk.

sterile   Free from living organisms.

tainted milk   Milk that's not suited to making quality cheese due to the animal's diet.

tartaric acid   An acid which occurs naturally in grapes.

thermophilic bacteria   Bacteria that grows best at higher temperatures of 95°F to 105°F.

Tomme press   A simple cheese press used to form a traditional round shape roughly 7 inches in diameter and 3 inches thick.

ultrapasteurized   Subjected to pasteurization at higher-than-normal temperatures in order to extend shelf life.

USDA   Acronym for the United States Department of Agriculture, comprised of many agencies charged with different tasks related to agriculture and food supply.

vegetarian   A dietary choice that excludes meat and animal products but allows the consumption of dairy products.

whey   The liquid portion of milk after the curds have been separated from it.

Resources

Now that you've begun your cheese-making journey, where can you find more information and support on related issues? Many resources are available in the form of websites and books. This appendix will provide you with suggestions on where to go for further information and instruction.

Books

Amrein-Boyes, Debra. *200 Easy Homemade Cheese Recipes*. Toronto: Robert Rose, 2009.

Carroll, Ricki. *Home Cheese Making*. North Adams, MA: Storey Publishing, 2002.

Jenkins, Steven. *Cheese Primer*. New York: Workman Publishing, 1996.

Kindstedt, Paul, of the Vermont Cheese Council. *American Farmstead Cheese*. White River Junction, VT: Chelsea Green Publishing, 2005.

Law, Berry A. *Technology of Cheesemaking*. Sheffield, UK: Sheffield Academic Press, 1999.

Peters-Morris, Margaret. *The Cheesemaker's Manual*. Winchester, Ontario, Canada: Glengarry Cheesemaking, 2003.

Online

The following links include the locations of reliable sources for milk in your area, the classifications of cheese and the definitions of terms that crop up in cheese making, and the tools you'll need to make cheese.

Sources for Milk

www.eatwild.com

www.smalldairy.com

www.realmilk.com/where.html

www.realmilk.com/cowfarmshare.html

Classifications and Definitions

http://naldr.nal.usda.gov/NALWeb/Agricola_Link.asp?Accession=CAT87210559

www.access.gpo.gov/nara/cfr/waisidx_06/21cfr131_06.html

www.cheesesociety.org

Supplies

www.leeners.com

www.cheesemaking.com

The Cheesemaker's Worksheet

CHEESEMAKER'S WORKSHEET Production Date _____ Type of Cheese _____

DETAILS OF THE MILK USED	INGREDIENT DETAILS	FORMULATION COMMENTS AND NOTES
Type of Milk _____	Batch Size _____	
Milk Source _____	1st Culture _____	
Pasteurized _____	2nd Culture _____	
Homogenized _____	Coagulant _____	
Fat Content _____	Others _____	

	OPERATION	TIME - TEMPERATURE - FACTORS	FORMULATION COMMENTS AND NOTES
STANDARDIZE	Prepare Cheese Milk		
	Begin Heating		
ACIDIFICATION	Primary Acidification		
	Secondary Culture		
	Other Additives		
GEL DEVELOPMENT	Coagulating Addition		
	Onset of Flocculation		
	Clean Break		
CURD PROCESSING	Cutting		
	Cooking		
	Draining		
	Cheddaring		
	Salting		
PRESSING / SHAPING	Schedule of Weights & Times		
RIND PREPARATION	Brining		
	Mold Application		
AGING	Starting Storage Conditions		
	Final Storage Conditions		

Leeners
9293 Olde Eight Road, Northfield, Ohio 44067
800-543-3697

Index

CHECK OUT THESE BEST-SELLERS

More than 450 titles available at booksellers and online retailers everywhere!

978-1-59257-115-4

978-1-59257-900-6

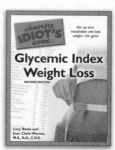

978-1-59257-855-9

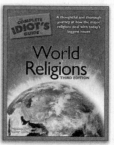

978-1-59257-222-9

978-1-59257-957-0

978-1-59257-785-9

978-1-59257-471-1

978-1-59257-483-4

978-1-59257-883-2

978-1-59257-966-2

978-1-59257-908-2

978-1-59257-786-6

978-1-59257-954-9

978-1-59257-437-7

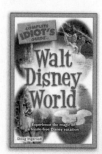

978-1-59257-888-7

ALPHA idiotsguides.com